CAMBRIDGE LIBRARY COLLECTION

Books of enduring scholarly value

Literary studies

This series provides a high-quality selection of early printings of literary works, textual editions, anthologies and literary criticism which are of lasting scholarly interest. Ranging from Old English to Shakespeare to early twentieth-century work from around the world, these books offer a valuable resource for scholars in reception history, textual editing, and literary studies.

College Plays

George Charles Moore Smith (1858–1940) was a renowned literary scholar who graduated from St John's College, Cambridge, with a first-class degree in the classics in 1881. In 1896 he was made professor of English language and literature at Firth College, Sheffield, and he played a key role in building up the social and academic position of the institution after it became the University of Sheffield in 1905. *College Plays Performed in the University of Cambridge* (1923) includes a chronological table of the Latin plays performed by scholars at the university in the sixteenth and seventeenth centuries. The study also contains Moore Smith's 48-page introduction along with an appendix of actor lists. The introduction provides useful context to sixteenth- and seventeenth-century literary and theatrical culture at the University of Cambridge, discussing both the 'outlines of [the plays] histories' and the 'manner of [their] production'.

T0382049

Cambridge University Press has long been a pioneer in the reissuing of out-of-print titles from its own backlist, producing digital reprints of books that are still sought after by scholars and students but could not be reprinted economically using traditional technology. The Cambridge Library Collection extends this activity to a wider range of books which are still of importance to researchers and professionals, either for the source material they contain, or as landmarks in the history of their academic discipline.

Drawing from the world-renowned collections in the Cambridge University Library, and guided by the advice of experts in each subject area, Cambridge University Press is using state-of-the-art scanning machines in its own Printing House to capture the content of each book selected for inclusion. The files are processed to give a consistently clear, crisp image, and the books finished to the high quality standard for which the Press is recognised around the world. The latest print-on-demand technology ensures that the books will remain available indefinitely, and that orders for single or multiple copies can quickly be supplied.

The Cambridge Library Collection will bring back to life books of enduring scholarly value (including out-of-copyright works originally issued by other publishers) across a wide range of disciplines in the humanities and social sciences and in science and technology.

College Plays

Performed in the University of Cambridge

George Charles Moore Smith

CAMBRIDGE UNIVERSITY PRESS

Cambridge, New York, Melbourne, Madrid, Cape Town, Singapore,
São Paolo, Delhi, Dubai, Tokyo

Published in the United States of America by Cambridge University Press, New York

www.cambridge.org
Information on this title: www.cambridge.org/9781108008891

This edition first published 1923
This digitally printed version 2010

ISBN 978-1-108-00889-1 Paperback

COLLEGE PLAYS

CAMBRIDGE UNIVERSITY PRESS

C. F. CLAY, MANAGER

LONDON : FETTER LANE, E.C. 4

NEW YORK : THE MACMILLAN CO.

BOMBAY
CALCUTTA } MACMILLAN AND CO., LTD
MADRAS

TORONTO : THE MACMILLAN CO. OF
CANADA, LTD

TOKYO : MARUZEN-KABUSHIKI-KAISHA

COLLEGE PLAYS

PERFORMED IN THE
UNIVERSITY OF CAMBRIDGE

By G. C. MOORE SMITH

CAMBRIDGE
AT THE UNIVERSITY PRESS
1923

PREFACE

THE following pages contain the results of work done for the most part a good many years ago. They illustrate the references to plays in the bursarial accounts of the Cambridge colleges, which were transcribed at the same time and which are to be published shortly by the Malone Society.

They are also supplementary to Dr F. S. Boas' standard work *University Drama in the Tudor Age* (1914) and to the same author's chapter on University Plays in the *Cambridge History of English Literature* with its appended Bibliography. It has been my endeavour not to repeat what has been so well said by Dr Boas. But perhaps in what has been left to me to say here, there is still something which may be of service to future historians of the University Drama. Much of it I know is tentative and open to correction. But the subject is one on which much has yet to be done.

In the Malone volume I have expressed my gratitude to the many officers of colleges whose ungrudging assistance made my work so pleasant and without which it could not have been done at all.

G. C. M. S.

February 1923

CONTENTS

CAMBRIDGE PLAYS

I

OUTLINES OF THEIR HISTORY

OUR chief source of knowledge in regard to the acting of plays in the different colleges of the University of Cambridge apart from that derived from the plays themselves printed or in MS. is the Bursarial Accounts. Unfortunately however this source often fails us. At St John's there are no college accounts extant of earlier date than 1555 and so we have no record of the performance of the plays seen in the college hall by Ascham. At Caius there are no accounts before 1609, though we know of the performance of a play at Caius just thirty years earlier. Even where the accounts exist, their mention of performances known to us from other sources is only haphazard, especially after the earliest period. And where they do mention a performance, more often than not they omit the name of the play.

Long before plays were acted by members of the University in their several colleges, players, musicians and jesters of the town or strollers attached to some great household frequently made their appearance and received an acknowledgement from the colleges of the performances they gave. Entries of such payments are found in the accounts of King's Hall (preserved in Trinity College) as early as Michaelmas 1448–1449 (27 Henry VI).

Payments to the town-waits ('mimis,' 'tibicinibus')

of Cambridge occur in various college accounts annually throughout the whole period [1]. They probably received further payment when called upon, as they frequently were, to provide music at college plays [2].

The earliest evidence of the production of plays by the members of a college themselves is found in the accounts of King's College. Thus:

1482–83: 'Item sol. Goldyng pro vestimentis per eundem emptis pro lusoribus erga primum diem Januarij   xxᵈ
Item sol. Goldyng & Suthey pro expensis circa ludos in festo Natalis dni   vijˢ ijᵈ'

[1] The Waits held their office by election by the town. There were three of them. Cooper, *Annals*, II, 62, quotes a minute from the Corporation Day Book showing that on Hock Day (May) 1552 the Commoners of Cambridge agreed that John Richemond and John Clerke should continue waits and the Town minstrels during good behaviour and that Benet Pryme should be the third if he would. This was apparently an unsuccessful attempt to patch up a quarrel, as Mere on 2nd Feb. 1556/7 (see J. Lamb, *Letters, Statutes, etc.*, 1838) while mentioning that Benet Pryme and his men were present at King's College when Mere dined there, distinguishes them clearly from the waits of the town. The same distinction is made in the accounts of the Steward of Trinity College for 1557–8: 'gyuen in rewarde vnto wydowe prymes men both for shewes & playes & yᵉ whayttes rewarde—xxˢ.'
As late as 1820 the waits of Westminster held office under the High Constable and Court of Burgesses and allowed of no interlopers (Chambers' *Book of Days*, II, 743).
[2] Cp. the accounts of Christ's, 1531, 1532, 1553, 1559, King's, 1552 (Benet Pryme), 1576, Trinity, 1561, 1669, Corpus, 1576.

1484–85: '(Liber Communarum. Term. Nativ. 5th week.) Item pro communis ij pictorum per totam septimaniam pro le disgysyns erga festum purificationis xvj^d

ibid. 6th week. Item pro communis duorum pictorum per v. dies pro-le disgysyng xx^d'

1496–97: 'Item sol. m. Stalis pro expensis suis circa ludos tempore natalis dni anno xii° xx^s'

1508–09: 'Item xiij° die Januarij m. Stephins pro lusu tempore Natalis dni xx^s'

1510–11: 'Item m. West pro lusu in tempore Natalis dni xx^s'

1535–36: 'Item in Regardis datis Mro Viceproposito pro supervisione ludorum in tempore Natalis dni xx^s'

1536–37: 'Item in Regardis datis Mro Rivete pro supervisione Ludorum in tempore Natalis dni xx^s'

1541–42: 'Item pro supervisione ludorum hoc anno xx^s'

1544–45: 'Item pro supervisione ludi natalis xx^s'

1545–46: 'Item m. Parkyn pro expensis suis circa ludos natalicios xx^s'

1548–49: 'Item pro supervisione ludorum tempore natalis lvij^s vij^d'

At King's College down to this date we have no information of the character of the plays performed. Such indications we get first in two items of the accounts of King's Hall.

1510–11: 'Item solutum est pro comedia Terentij in Ludo vi^s viij^d'

1516–17: 'Item in regardis m^{ro} thrope pro ludo puerorum suorum therencij iij^s iiij^d'

Mr Thrope was 'locum tenens' or vice-master of King's Hall at this time, the master being apparently non-resident. The second item makes it clear that his

pupils presented a play of Terence in the winter of
1516–17, and, as Terence was not likely to be acted
by strolling players, we may conclude that the performance in 1510–11 was also given by undergraduates of King's Hall.

Although the accounts of King's Hall are preserved
down to the year 1543 when it was about to be dis-
solved, they contain no other mention of plays acted
by members of the Hall. It is therefore extremely
fortunate that they show that Terence was acted in
Cambridge as early as 1510 and that the Renaissance
influence was by that date already at work. No doubt
it was some time before this influence became pre-
dominant. The plays which Bale assigns to Thomas
Artour, fellow of St John's 1520–1532, to judge by
their titles (*Microcosmus* and *Mundus Plumbeus*) par-
took of the character of Moralities. But at Christmas
1536 Aristophanes' *Plutus* was acted at St John's in
Greek with the Erasmian pronunciation and about
1540 Thomas Watson's Latin tragedy *Absalon*, an
imitation of the tragedies of Seneca, was acted at the
same college.

Aristophanes' *Pax* was given at Trinity in Greek,
probably at Christmas 1546, the first Christmas in
the life of the college. It must have been either
that Christmas or after 1553 that Christopherson's
Jephthes was played, if it was ever played at all, i.e.
at Trinity. The Greek version is extant in two manu-
scripts, to be dated *c.* 1544[1]: the Latin version, if it

1 Cp. Boas, *University Drama*, p. 45.

ever existed, is lost. After this we hear no more of plays in Greek, but the original Latin comedies of Plautus and Terence and the original Latin tragedies of Seneca continued to be given on college stages at least down to 1583.

Dr Boas' book gives such an admirable account of the development of the Academic drama till 1603 that it will not be necessary to do more than remind his readers of the main features, and add a few supplementary touches.

Seneca's tragedies and Plautus and Terence's comedies were gradually replaced on college stages by modern imitations of them—borrowed or original —and by other forms of drama, generally in Latin, occasionally in English. Tragic and serious subjects were provided by the Bible, and Cambridge saw Ziegler's (?) *Heli* (1548), Christopherson's *Jephthes* (1546 or 1555–6?), Birck's (?) *Sapientia Solomonis* (1559–60), Buchanan's (?) *Baptistes* and Foxe's *Christus Triumphans* (1562–3), Udall's *Ezechias* (in English) (1564), Legge's (perhaps Buchanan's) *Jephthes* (1566). Protestantism found a controversial weapon in Naogeorgus' *Pammachius* (1545) and in the show of *The Imprisoned Bishops* (1564). The 'Prodigal Son' plays of the continent seemed to provide edification for young students and they too were staged on our boards: *Hypocrisis* in 1548/9, *Acolastus* in 1560–1, *Asotus* in 1565–6.

English history furnished its lessons of Senecan morality when Dr Legge's *Richardus Tertius* in three actions was presented at St John's in the spring of 1578/9 [1].

Cambridge, however, as Dr Boas has pointed out, was especially given to Romantic Comedy. In this genre it composed its own plays, though generally on the basis of some Italian play or story. One is inclined to date the beginnings of Italian influence in the last quarter of the 16th century: certainly *Gammer Gurton's Needle* (*c.* 1552?) knows nothing of it, but is a farcical comedy of English invention owing a little of its form to Plautus. Yet there is evidence hard to get over, evidence which was not known to Dr Boas, that before *Gammer Gurton* was written, the Italian influence had already operated. The play *Lælia,* based on a French translation of *Gli Ingannati,* has been assigned to the year 1594/5 when it was acted at Queens' College before the Earl of Essex and other noblemen. Yet among the archives of Queens' there is a paper of the date 1546/7 which is headed 'New made garmentes at the comœdie of Lælia Modenas.' One cannot say that the play as we know it had not been rewritten later. But the fact that it was produced at Queens' College in 1594/5 suggests that those responsible for it then had the old Queens' play before them. And one may ask, if they had not had it, would they have been likely to hit on a foreign play for imitation written and printed so many years earlier?

[1] Reference to the College accounts will make it almost certain that this date and not 1579/80, as generally given, is the right one.

Assuming however that a Latin version of the Lælia story was produced in 1546/7, there is a gap in time before the next comedies known to us—namely, Fraunce's *Victoria* (*c*. 1579), *Hymenæus* of about the same date and the three plays of *c*. 1597 (introduced by the revived *Lælia* of 1594/5), *Silvanus, Hispanus,* and *Machiavellus.* All five were produced at St John's.

Meanwhile plays had been written in which the interest was sought in topical satire. They were headed by *Pedantius* (1581), the author of which is now ascertained to have been Edward Forset, Fellow of Trinity[1]. Its butt was Gabriel Harvey. The three *Parnassus* plays of St John's College satirizing in English verse the woeful prospects of the poor student were acted between 1598 and 1602. In 1599 the coarse but brilliant *Club Law* embodied the contempt and hatred of young University men for the civic authorities of Cambridge—thus taking up again a theme which had been treated in 1582/3 by one Mudde of Pembroke in a little play now lost.

Meanwhile another Italian genre, Pastoral, had made its appearance with a Latin version of L. Groto's *Pentimento Amoroso, Parthenia,* and another of Guarini's *Pastor Fido, Pastor Fidus* (*c*. 1595–1600?). Two writers within the next twenty years were conspicuous pastoralists, Phineas Fletcher, who produced an English comedy at King's in 1606, and his English piscatory, *Sicelides,* in 1614/5, and Dr Samuel Brooke of Trinity whose *Scyros* (a version

[1] See *Times Literary Supplement,* 10 Oct. 1918.

of Bonarelli's *Filli di Sciro*) was acted in 1612/3 before Prince Charles and the Elector Palatine, and whose *Melanthe* entertained King James in 1614/5.

In the first twenty years of the 17th century there was a curious revival of the morality-type of play, in which the characters were abstract conceptions. It was perhaps suggested by the Oxford play *Bellum Grammaticale*, which had an Oxford successor in Zouch's *Fallacy* (called in its revised form *The Sophister*). Three Cambridge plays of this type, all in English, are possibly all the work of Thomas Tomkis of Trinity (author of the English comedy *Albumazar* acted before King James in 1614/5). These are *Lingua*, probably produced as early as 1602, the imperfect *Locus, Corpus*, etc., *c.* 1604/5, and *Pathomachia* (perhaps never acted), (*c.* 1617). We may also more doubtfully assign to Tomkis the two shows, *Band, Cuffe and Ruffe* (entitled in its revised form *Exchange Ware*) and *Worke for Cutlers*. They were both printed in 1615, the former being entered on the Stat. Reg. as 'A Dialogue between Ruffe, Cuffe and Band' to Miles Patricke, 10 Feb. 1614/5, the second on 4 July 1615. Other plays of this type are in Latin, such as the anonymous play, *Microcosmus*, etc. (Trinity MS. R. 10. 4), *Stoicus Vapulans* acted at St John's in 1618, and *Fucus* (Queens' 1622/3). Meanwhile romantic and satirical comedy continued its course with *Leander* (1598/9 and 1602/3) and *Labyrinthus* (1602/3)—both by Walter Hawkesworth of Trinity, *Adelphe* (1611/2) by S. Brooke of Trinity, *Albumazar* (1614/5) by T. Tomkis of Trinity, *Euribates* (?1616) by Aquila Cruso of Caius, *Fortunia* (or *Susenbrotus*)—acted by Trinity men before King James and Prince Charles in 1616, perhaps at Royston—*Fraus Honesta* by Edmund Stub, Trinity (1618/9 and 1629), *Pseudomagia* by W. Mewe, Emmanuel (*c.* 1625), *Cancer* (of unknown date and college), *Paria* by T. Vincent of Trinity acted before King Charles 1627/8—the two last adapted respectively from L. Salviati's *Il Granchio* and E. Luchetti's *Le duc Sorelle Rivali*,—P. Hausted's *Senile Odium* (Queens', ?1628/9)—possibly *Senilis Amor* (*c.* 1635/6).

Satire of Common Lawyers, especially of the Recorder of Cambridge, had found expression in *Ignoramus*, acted before King James twice in 1615, satire of Jesuits and Puritans in J. Hacket's *Loiola,* acted at Trinity before King James in 1622/3, and in the semi-morality *Fucus Histriomastix* by R. Ward of Queens', acted before the king at Newmarket a week or two later. The anti-Puritan spirit appears also in Hausted's *Rivall Friends*, 1631/2, W. Johnson's *Valetudinarium* (Queens', 1637/8) and A. Cowley's *Naufragium Joculare* (Trinity, 1638/9). Between 1626 and 1631 we must put Randolph's witty productions, *Aristippus, The Conceited Peddler, The Entertainment* (*Muses Looking-Glasse*), *Hey for Honesty*, etc. *Aristippus* was presented at Trinity 'in a private shew,' *The Conceited Peddler* 'in a strange shew'; it does not appear if *Hey for Honesty* was ever acted. Hausted's *Rivall Friends*, and Randolph's *Jealous Lovers*, were acted before King Charles and Queen Mary in 1631/2, A. Cowley's *The Guardian* before Prince Charles in 1641/2. All three are of course in English. It is hard to decide if the anonymous *Fraus Pia*, supposing it to be a Cambridge play, dates from this time or from the Restoration.

Before the outbreak of Civil War, most colleges had ceased to give plays. After 1620 we hear no more of plays at St John's, so famous for its plays in earlier times: no more of the more sporadic performances which used to take place at King's, Jesus, Christ's, Peterhouse, Caius. Trinity and Queens' seem to have been the only colleges left in which plays were still performed with distinction. Queens' was, as we have seen, especially active in the thirties when it had Peter Hausted to set against Tom Randolph of Trinity. Before the end of the decade it had built itself a Comedy House:

> Alas regardless of their doom
> The little victims play.

In 1642 Puritanism, which the prologue of *Fucus* (1622/3) had described as striving

ut comœdias quotannis parturientem Academiam abortum facere cogeret,

at last achieved its purpose. For eighteen years no more plays were presented and even the Restoration brought but a flickering revival.

It is time to turn back from a résumé of the types

of play acted in Cambridge to a consideration of the
aspect in which college plays were regarded at
different periods and by different people. The earlier
humanists, such as Ascham, saw in them a potent
educational instrument, and had no scruples about
their effect on morals. The redoubtable Puritan
T. Cartwright produced *Trinummus* at Trinity early
in 1564. The German W. Soone was at Cambridge
some years before 1575. At that time the humanistic
side of the performances was still the prominent one.
When he thought of the plays that beguiled the long
evenings of January, February and March, he had
in his mind tragedies of Sophocles, Euripides and
Seneca, comedies of Aristophanes, Plautus and
Terence. In his eyes they were acted with rare
ability and set forth with magnificence [1]. But already
changes were in progress. The classical interest
declined; the new interest in Italian romance grew
stronger. Plays may have become more amusing,
but they certainly became less edifying. Tragedy
gradually ceased to be played. The performances
became more and more expensive. And the ever-
growing body of Puritan opinion saw more evil than
good in play-acting and worked for its abolition. As
early as 27 Feb. 1564/5 we find the Vice-Chancellor
informing the Archbishop of Canterbury that

one in Christs and some in St Johns will be hardly
brought to wear surplyses, and ii or iii in Trinitie

[1] See his account of Cambridge in vol. II of
G. Braunius' *De præcipuis totius vniversi vrbibus,*
liber secundus. Dated from Cologne, 1575.

college thynke it very unseeming yt Christians sholde playe or be present at any prophane comædies or tragædies[1].

The performances were denounced from the pulpit, even the pulpit of St Mary's. On Ash Wednesday 1585/6, John Smith, M.A., in a sermon 'ad clerum' declared that

the plays at Saturday and Sunday at night were breaches of the Christian Sabbath. On Sunday for they were at it before the sun was set. On Saturday for disabling of their bodies for the sabbath duties[2].

Stephen Gosson in his *Playes confuted in five actions* (? 1590) represents a more extreme opinion still:

So subtill is the devill, that under the colour of recreation in London and of exercise of learning in the Universities, by seeing of playes, he maketh us to join with the Gentiles in their corruptions[3].

The sustained attack of John Rainolds in his controversy with Gager at Oxford in 1592–5 and in his book *Th' Overthrow of Stage-Playes*, 1599, is fully treated by Dr Boas[4].

In vain does Heywood in 1612 call on the memories of his past Cambridge days and reassert the old humanist defence of academical plays[5]. He had the older men of the university on his side, but he has himself heard men of a newer school 'as liberally tax the exercises performed in their colleges as these

[1] Cooper, *Annals*, II, 213.
[2] Cooper, *Annals*, II, 415.
[3] Quoted in *Retrospective Review*, XII, 20.
[4] *University Drama, passim.*
[5] See Boas, *ibid.* p. 350.

acted on our public stages.' And Prynne in 1633 is justified in saying that college plays were then, owing to the expenses of time and money and their falling under religious condemnation in common with plays in general, less frequent than they had been in former times: 'only practised in some private houses [i.e. colleges] perchance once in three or four years, and that by the particular statutes of those houses made in times of Popery'[1].

[1] *Histriomastix* (1633), p. 490: 'If any here Object: That our Vniversities approve of private Stage-playes acted by Schollers in private Colledges: therefore these Playes are not so intolerably evill in Their opinions. I answer; that our Vniversities though they tolerate and connive at, yet they give no publike approbation to these private Enterludes, which are not generally received into all Colledges, but onely practised in some private houses (perchance once in three or foure yeeres;) and that by the particular Statutes of those houses made in times of Popery, which require some Latine Comedies, for learning-sake onely, to bee acted now and then: Which Playes as they are composed "for* the most part by idle braines, who affect not better studies; and acted (as I.G.) informes us, by Gentle-bloods, and lusty Swash-bucklers, who preferre an ounce of vaine-glory, ostentation and strutting on the Stage, before a pound of learning; or by such who are sent to the University, not so much to obtaine knowledge, as to keepe them from the common ryot of Gentlemen in these dayes; .. their spectators for the most part being such as both Poets and Actors are; even such as reckon no more of their studies, then spend-all Gentlemen of their cast-suites; So the graver, better and more studious sort,

* I.G. his Refutation of the Apologie for Actors, page 17, whose words I here recite. [I.G. according to the British Museum Catalogue is John Greene.]

Nor were the plays that were now acted of a kind calculated to propitiate the Puritan. Some verses written after the performances of *Ignoramus* in 1615 point out the change:

> Where Tragedies of Sovereigntie & State
> Were staged acting Kinges & princes fate,
> Where witty Comedies abhorring gall
> Were exercised in each Colledge hall,
> There there (o shame) nought now in steade of these
> But Pasquilles grosse & carrion jestes doe please.
> Whose lofty Cothurnes Sophocles did passe
> She nowe turnes Tarleton with her Cumane asse:
> Dulman & Ignoramus be her theames
> in steade of Phœbus & his tragicke threnes[1].

The young Milton, as he tells us, when witnessing some performance during his Cambridge days, *c.* 1624–30, felt only disgust at seeing men intended for Holy Orders:

writhing and unboning their clergy limbs to all the antick and dishonest gestures of Trincaloes, buffoons, and bawds; prostituting the shame of that ministry, which they had, or were near having, to the eyes of courtiers and court ladies, their grooms and mademoiselles.

The Puritan ascendancy stopped play-acting in colleges for eighteen years, and when the Restoration came, the old impetus at Queens' College had died

especially Divines...condemne them, censure them, come not at them." Neither are these Playes so frequent now as they have beene in former times, by reason of those mischiefes, "those expences of time and mony which they occasion, and that affinity they have with common Stage-playes which all ages..and these our Vniversities have solemnely condemned."'

[1] *Add. MS.* 23,723.

away. Only one college was faithful to the old tradition.

Trinity College alone seems to have set itself to rival or eclipse the theatrical triumphs of the past, but we are not aware that even Trinity found a new dramatist.

In 1662 Jonson's *Silent Woman* seems to have been given, probably in English[1], and on the following night Brooke's *Adelphe* was revived. The prologue suggests even that new plays were prohibited:

> Novam ideo iam quia nec libet *nec licet,*
> Vetustam ecce vobis exhibemus fabulam.

In 1663 a performance was given before the Duke of Monmouth, but we know not of what play: another unknown comedy was presented in 1664, and two comedies in 1665. In 1669 *Adelphe* seems to have been revived once more, and to have had two performances, that on May 1st being in honour of Cosmo de Medicis, Prince of Tuscany. Of this we have an account by a member of the Prince's suite:

The evening coming on, his highness was introduced into the theatre, a room rather small than spacious, where was represented by the scholars a Latin comedy, which pleased more by the elegance of the dresses, the ease and gracefulness of the actors, than by their elocution, which was very difficult to understand, without being accustomed to the accent. The story of the comedy was as follows: A merchant of Nola &c.... The comedy concludes in the midst of rejoicings with a ball, which was managed with great elegance[2].

[1] Epilogue to *Adelphe*. Pepys saw *The Silent Woman* in London on Jan. 7 and May 25, 1661.

[2] Account by Count Lorenzo Magalotti, quoted in Cooper, *Annals*, III, 533.

Similarly in 1670 an unknown comedy was performed twice, once before the University, once before the Duke of Ormond. Finally in 1670 a comedy was prepared for the Prince of Orange (afterwards William III) but he did not come, and it was given to the University only.

Trinity's energies now seem to have been exhausted. Academic drama, beginning its course with Seneca, Plautus and Terence, as an instrument of education had become at last the mere amusement of an evening, and even so had died. Joshua Barnes of Emmanuel wrote some plays about 1675, one of which *The Academie or The Cambridge Dunns* was performed on June 28th, 1675, and June 26th, 1676, but this was a sporadic effort like that of Christopher Smart of Pembroke with his *Grateful Fair* of 1745-7. About 1837 we are told that 'an English play was acted in one of the halls with the sanction of the Master of the College and the Chancellor of the University'[1], but of this performance we know no more. The records of the A.D.C., the Footlights and the Thespids, and the Marlowe Society, and the great series of Greek plays which began in 1882, have little in common with those of the college performances of three and four centuries ago.

[1] *Cambridge Portfolio*, I, 111, 112 (1840).

II

MANNER OF PRODUCTION OF
COLLEGE PLAYS

THE PRODUCERS

THE first question that arises is this: What was
the connexion, if any, between the college plays
produced in the 16th and 17th centuries and the
institution known as the 'Christmas Lord'?

Dr Boas tells us that at Merton College, Oxford, a
Christmas Lord, 'Rex Fabarum' as he was there
called, was appointed as early as 1485 'per antiquam
consuetudinem'[1]. According to Wood, whom Dr
Boas quotes, he was the senior fellow that had not
borne the office, and had from Christmas to Candlemas a mock-authority over his juniors. Wood does
not assign to the 'Rex Fabarum' the duty of providing
plays or shows: but from a decree of the Dean and
Chapter of Christ Church of Dec. 12th, 1554, it
seems that the annual comedies and tragedies were
produced by 'the Lord.' (Dr Boas tells me however
that it was the two Censors who were usually responsible for them and paid the accounts.) At St
John's College, Oxford—at least when the office of
Christmas Lord was filled again after 30 years inter-
mission in 1607—it also fell to this officer to produce
tragedies and comedies. Dr Boas suggests what is
probably the true account of the matter, that the
production of tragedies and comedies, an outcome
of the Renaissance, had been attached to the office

[1] P. 5.

of the Christmas Lord, though as a burlesque ruler
he still kept some characteristics which had belonged
to his office in pre-Renaissance times.

At Cambridge, perhaps, this fusion never took
place. The Christmas Lord held sway in certain
colleges, but the office of providing plays for a
serious purpose was assigned to others.

First as to the Christmas Lord.

The statutes of St John's of 1545 prescribe that
at Christmas time every fellow in his turn 'dominum
agat,' and should write his statutes in Greek or Latin
verse and should produce at least six dialogues or
shows before Twelfth Day. He should receive 20*s*.
for his expenses. But it is noteworthy that the earlier
statutes of the college of 1516, 1524 and 1530 make
no mention of a Christmas Lord nor do the later
statutes of 1560. Again, while according to Warton [1]
'the original draft of the Statutes of Trinity College'
(does he mean the Statutes of 1546?) has a chapter
'De Præfecto Ludorum qui Imperator dicitur,' the
statutes of 1560 in place of this chapter have another
providing for plays to be produced by other hands.

According to John Dee, the Trinity Lord received
the title Imperator in the first year of the existence
of the college (1546) [2]. King's College had its 'King,'
Corpus perhaps its 'Dean' [3]. Christ's had its Lord as

[1] See Cooper, *Annals*, II, 112.
[2] Boas, *University Drama*, p. 9.
[3] The college decreed in 1622/3: 'Decanum in Ferijs
Natalitijs nullum deinceps fore.'

early as 1539/40 when 8*s*. 8*d*. was 'expe*n*dyde by the Lorde in Chrystymas for players garme*n*tes.'

It was the custom for these officers to visit other colleges and present their shows there. Thus the Queens' College accounts under 8 Jan. 1547/8 have the item: 'pro le sukket marmaled carawys cakes pro vino et pomis qu*um* rex regalis collegij, Imperator [sc. Trinitatis collegii] et reliqui veniebant huc.. xij* iiij*d*,' and under 14 Jan. 1548/9: 'domino Harryson p*ro* exceptione Legatorum qui aderant a collegijs regis et trinitatis..iiij* viij*d*.' On the 2nd July following King Edward VI's Visitors issued an injunction that henceforth no one was to be appointed Dominus Ludorum in any college at Christmas[1], but the injunction was disobeyed, at any rate after the end of the reign.

In 1552/3 at Christ's College 2*d*. was 'paid for sedge wha*n* ye Christemas Lords came at candlemas to ye colledge with shewes.'

In 1552–3 there is an item in the Trinity accounts: 'Mr Rooke for his alowance beyng lord in Christyn-mas—xl*s*' and one in the year 1554–5: 'payd vnto Mr Thulace, being the Lord of Christianmesse, for certayn charges whytche he dyd require for—viij*s*' as well as a sum to 'Wyllm̄ Carpenter,' 'for makyn a Clubb for the lord of Christianmesse,' and a number of other charges 'Pro Domino Ludorum.'

In 1555–6 Christ's College spent 25*s*. 'at a shew goynge to ye Kynges college,' and on 27 Dec. 1556,

[1] Cooper, *Annals*, II, 32.

'the lorde of Christes College came Christmas lyke' to Peterhouse 'with a drum before hym,' etc.[1]

In that same winter B. Doddington, then a young fellow of St John's, had 20*s*. allowed him as Lord in Christmas[2]. 'Mr Deye' was 'Kynge' at King's at Christmas 1556–7 as we learn from Mere's Diary.

Payments were made at Christ's to 'Mr Jesoppe being Lord' and 'to the Lord at Christemas' in 1557–8 and 1558–9 while at St John's in 1557–8 (the item comes in the last quarter, so probably refers to the Christmas of 1558) there is a payment: 'to Mr barnesdall for beynge lord. . xx^s' and one: 'for mendynge ye drum and other of my lords Jewells.' The institution lingered on into the 17th century. In a sermon preached at St Mary's on 21 Dec. 1609, William Ames, Fellow of Christ's, inveighed 'against the liberty taken at that time, especially in such colleges who had lords of misrule'[3].

Meanwhile the plays, considered so valuable an instrument of education, were entrusted at Cambridge to other hands than those of the madcap Christmas Lord. When we first hear of Terence being acted at King's Hall, a payment is made by the Hall for the expenses to a prominent fellow, Mr Thrope. And the early accounts of King's College show that a payment was made, probably annually, to a fellow of the College 'pro supervisione ludorum.'

The same statutes of 1545 which provide that at

[1] Cooper, *Ann.* II, 111.   [2] College accounts.
[3] Cooper, *Ann.* III, 34.

St John's every fellow should in turn at Christmas 'act the lord,' also provide (cap. xxvi) that the other comedies and tragedies to be acted between Twelfth Day and Lent should be provided by the several lecturers and examiners in turn. Even in the four short vacations the students were to be occupied among other things in acting comedies and tragedies (cap. xx). The statutes of Queens' of 1546 provide that two comedies or tragedies should be produced by the Greek lecturer and the examiner between Dec. 20th and Ash Wednesday; those of Trinity of 1560 that the nine lecturers should give five plays in the twelve days of Christmas. The statutes of Trinity, St John's and Queens', then, breathe the humanistic spirit of faith in the educational uses of play-acting. It is noticeable that those of Gonville and Caius College reflect the more conservative and doubtful attitude of its second founder. To John Caius college plays were a fact to be reckoned with, but they did not deserve much encouragement. He refers to them in cap. 53 of his Statutes (1574) only in regard to the dangers the college may incur from them whether acted within or without the walls, and the precautions thus necessitated:

Cap 53. *De custodia collegii.*

Constituimus etiam ut in omnibus concionibus, omnibus tragœdiis et comœdiis extra collegium habitis atque recitatis, omnibus nundinis, tres minimum socii domi sint et sex scholastici ex fundatione ad collegii custodiam: et ut sociorum unus cum scholasticis duobus divagetur per omnes collegii partes usque dum cæteri redierint, et excubias diligenter agat propter furta, incendia aut injurias externas omnino constituimus. Diligentiores autem fieri volumus, ubi quid in nostro collegio geratur, ob quod magna scholasticorum aut aliorum confluentia fuerit, ut in concionibus, comœdiis aut tragœdiis, quas privatas esse volumus, si quæ fuerint, propter turbas, et interdiu seu meridie propter infortunia.

If plays were given in Caius, they were to be 'private,' i.e. for members of the college only, and they were to be given by daylight.

In accordance with the terms of the statutes, it would seem from the college accounts that the production of plays was undertaken by fellows of the college other than the Christmas Lord. Thus in the year 1556–7 when B. Doddington was Christmas Lord at St John's, a payment is made to a carpenter 'whan Mr Lakyn sette furth his playe.'

The fellow who 'set forth' the play was in many cases its author or adapter, but by no means invariably even where the play was a new one. Cp. the payment made at Trinity in 1642: 'to Mr Willis for Dᵉ Cooleys Comedy' [A. Cowley's play *The Guardian*].

The performers, so far as our evidence goes, were practically always members of the college in which the play was produced, masters of arts, bachelors or undergraduates: and the same is true of the author. Dr Legge, the author of *Richardus Tertius* acted at St John's in 1578/9, belonged indeed to another college, but we cannot point with certainty to another case which is parallel to this. If Bridges, and not

William Stevenson (see Boas, *Un. Drama*, pp. 83–7), was the author of *Gammer Gurton's Needle* this play was also written by a man who did not belong to the college in which it was performed. *Prima facie*, this goes against Bridges' authorship. Still more rash is it to ascribe the Parnassus Plays to a non-Johnian author on much slighter evidence. See Dr Boas' judicious remarks, *ibid*. p. 332 *n*. Some plays, intended for the amusement of royal or distinguished visitors, were really University, rather than College, productions, e.g. *Ignoramus*, acted before King James at Trinity in 1615. In this case the author belonged to Clare Hall, the actors were drawn chiefly from Clare, but also from other colleges, and the expenses were met by a subsidy levied on all the colleges of the University.

PLACE OF PERFORMANCE

We hear that at Jesus about 1567–9 plays were given in the college chapel, at St John's in 1568/9 there was a 'show' 'in the gallerie,' at Queens' in 1548/9 acting seems to have taken place 'in conclaui,' or, as in 1560/1, 'in cubiculo Præsidis.' But by far the most usual place of performance was the college hall. We remember Ascham's glowing reference to the appearance of St John's hall in play-time. He writes to his friend E. Raven on 1st Oct. 1550:

Sept. tricesimo Antverpiam venimus, Dii boni! non Brabantiæ, sed totius mundi ditissimum emporium. Splendida magnificaque structura sic eminet, ut eo modo superet omnes urbes quas ego vidi quemadmodum aula Divi Joannis theatrali more ornata post natalem seipsam superat[1].

Tabor, the University Registrary, describes the arrangements at the performance of *Ignoramus* before King James on 13th May 1615 in the hall of Trinity College:

The vice-chancellor took order for the placing of the university and strangers, not actors: at the lower end of the stage, the doctors; in a place next the stage, the regents and non-regents in gowns; in the body of the hall, other strangers according to their qualities, upon the scaffolds: the upper end of the hall, beyond the stage, was wholly reserved for the king and prince's followers and for the courtiers. About 8 of the clock the play began, and ended about one[2].

On the occasion of Queen Elizabeth's visit to Cambridge in 1564, the Hall of King's College proving unsuitable, the stage was erected at the Queen's expense in the ante-chapel. Behind it at the foot of the Rood-screen was a stand for officers of the court. The Queen ascended the stage by steps from the choir, and mounted to her own seat placed at the side of the stage by the south wall.

Queens' seems to have built itself a playhouse in 1638–39, which was probably hardly used: while Trinity, perhaps after 1660, erected a Comedy House near the back of the Master's Lodge, in which presumably all its plays were acted after that date.

Plays before royalty were occasionally given out of Cambridge: thus a play, perhaps *Susenbrotus* (otherwise called *Fortunia*), was given at Royston in 1615/6,

[1] *The Whole Works of R. Ascham*, ed. Giles, I, 212.
[2] *Ignoramus*, ed. Hawkins (1787), p. cxxi.

and *Fucus* at Newmarket in 1622/3. Perhaps it was at Newmarket that Hausted's *Rivall Friends* was given in 1631/2.

SPECTATORS

When a college play was given 'privatim,' only members of that college, we presume, would be present at the representation. At a 'public' performance, there would also be present invited guests such as the doctors of the University. Christ's College spent 32*s*. 3½*d*. in 1552–3 'towards yᵉ honest enterteynemente of yᵉ Worshippe of yᵉ towne & th' universitie which resorted to our colledge to see yᵉ plaies.' The St John's accounts (21 Feb. 1595) mention a payment to the apothecary (? for tobacco), 'when the Doctors were invited' (probably to the shows). Fuller in his well-known account of the performance of *Club Law* at Clare Hall (1599–1600) says that on that occasion the Mayor of Cambridge with his Brethren and their wives were invited to see themselves held up to scorn. A college hall would not ordinarily hold, one would suppose, many guests if part of it was taken up with a stage and if all the members of the college were present at the same time. Probably in most cases the play was performed once for the college and once 'before the University.' Probably admission was not regulated in regard to undergraduates of other colleges by invitation or ticket, but it was a case of first come, first served. Hence the frequent ebullitions of annoyance on the part of the excluded.

Lady visitors were probably not often among the spectators. But the epilogue of *Clytophon* addresses 'Spectatrices' and that of *Leander* has: 'petit Alphonsus vt obliscamini eius in Ardeliam | Contumelias, neque vereamini, vt erga vos, Spectatrices, si qua usque fuerit, | Itidem ingratus siet.' Most plays (e.g. *Ignoramus, Stoicus Vapulans, Loiola, Senile Odium*) seem to address themselves only to men.

THE STAGE-HOUSES

As to the stage-arrangements they followed the unified system of Latin comedy. There is no trace of the 'multiple scene.' Nor was there any change of scene—at any rate till a very late period. As many statements show, 'houses' were erected for the different groups into which the dramatis personæ were divided. Fraunce prefixed to his comedy now called *Victoria,* ? 1579, the direction:

Quatuor extruendæ sunt domus, nimirum Fidelis, 1ª, Fortunij, 2ª, Cornelij, 3ª, Octauiani, 4ª. Quin et sacellum quoddam erigendum est, in quo constituendum est Cardinalis cuiusdam Sepulchrum, ita efformatum, vt claudi aperirique possit. In Sacello autem Lampas ardens ponenda est.

Sometimes the list of dramatis personæ itself groups the characters by houses, e.g. in Peter Hausted's *Senile Odium*, acted at Queens' College (printed 1633):

Ex domo Theophili—Ex Monasterio Sanctæ Catharinæ, Ex domo Ludovici—Ex domo Tricongionis—A Foro.

or W. Johnson's *Valetudinarium*, acted in the same College in 1637/8 (Emm. MS. 1. 2. 32):

Ex domo Algidij—Ex hospitio S^{cti} Bartholomæi—
E Lupanario—A foro.

The dramatis personæ of W. Hawkesworth's
Labyrinthus acted at Trinity College 1602/3 are
grouped by houses in various MSS. But the houses
are rather curiously described as 'Domus dec. sup.,'
'Domus Bac in med.,' 'Domus dec. inferioris' (? the
House of the Senior Dean, of the Bachelors in
Medicine, of the Junior Dean), while characters not
assigned to one or other of these houses are grouped
as 'semper a foro.'

Does this imply that for the performance structures
or partitions already existing in the hall were adapted
to stage purposes and obviated the need of building
stage houses *ad hoc*? We know that when the plays
were given before Queen Elizabeth in King's College
Ante-Chapel in 1564 the side-chapels were used as
houses. It is noticeable that when this play *Labyrinthus*
was printed in 1636 the names were divided into four
groups, of which the last was described as 'semper è
foro,' but the other indications, probably because
they would be unintelligible to the non-academic
reader, were omitted.

The stage-directions for entrances and exits sometimes indicate the stage-houses, as those in *Cancer*
(printed 1648):

I. i.   'ex ædibus Rod.'
I. iii.   'Granchio ex ædibus suis.
           Rod. transit scenam.'
I. iv.   'Fantichus ex ædibus Sempronii.'

I. v.   'Fortunius ex ædibus Granchi.'
I. vii. 'Gallus puer ex ædibus suis.'
I. ix. ad fin. '[Gallus] exit in ædes Vrsiliæ.'

The play *Timon* edited by Dyce for the Shakespeare Society has an academic character and seems to borrow from *Pedantius*. But it has nothing which definitely connects it with Oxford or Cambridge and is anomalous from the point of view of a college play in its stage-directions 'one dore,' 'another dore.' The characters in *Antoninus Bassianus Caracalla* are divided into two groups 'ex una parte' and 'e regione.'

References to the building of 'houses' for the stage are found in the College accounts. Thus Queens':

1522–3: 'pro.. Teynternayles quibus firmabantur ornamenta edium in.. comedia   1½ᵈ'
1545–6: 'emi funiculum.. pro erigendis domibus.. comædiæ   8ᵈ'

Christ's (1551–2) in connexion with 'S. Stephenson play':

'to yᵉ carpenter for removing yᵉ tables in yᵉ haull & setting yᵉᵐ vp agein wᵗʰ yᵉ houses & other things paid   12ᵈ'
Trinity, 17º februarij 1557: 'To William Hardwyke for one dayes work in mending yᵉ joyned chayer, and in mending formes and makynge howses for yᵉ players 11ᵈ'
Corpus, 1581–2: 'To Lamb and Porter for making houses at the Comædie   20ᵈ'

The construction of a temple and of a 'heaven' is indicated in the following items from the accounts of Queens' College:

1540–1: 'Dowseo..eo die quo agebantur comediæ..

pro candelabro et phano ligneo conficiendis et pro loris
pro eisdem   12^d
  thomæ pictori pingenti phanum et pro coloribus
quibus usi sunt actores comediarum   18^d'
  1551–2: 'Joanni pople pro opera tridui in fabricanda
le frame pro cœlo ante ludos   3^s
  Item famulo kynge pro opera totidem dierum in
eadem machina exedificanda   3^s
  Item Jo. pople et famulo Kynge pro erectione cœli
in lusu d. Josselyn   20^d'

In the Queens' accounts of 1540–1 payment is
made 'pro 4 oblongis clauis quibus affigebantur
gradus quibus ascendebant ad scenam.' Were these
steps for the use of the actors only? or of visitors
permitted to sit on the stage?

OTHER STAGE REQUIREMENTS

Particular performances demanded particular pre-
parations. Thus we have a payment made by King's
College in 1552–3:

  paid to Thorpe for makynge thunder agaynst the
plays   4^s
  paid to Burwell for a drye ffatt to make the thunder
on   20^d

and some by Trinity College in 1669–70:

  for 18 yds of cloth for ye Oake Trees and ye Well
                                                          6^s 8^d
  for ye Oake-Trees Painting..2 hoops for the Well..

In 1668–9 Trinity paid £2. 18s. 'for sixteen yards
of green bays (baize) to cover ye stage.'

BOOKS OF THE PLAY

Before the play could be learnt, copies of it had
to be written out for the use of the actors. So at the

end of 1578 when *Richardus Tertius* was in preparation, we have payments in the accounts of St John's:

> for paper to write out yᵉ bookes for yᵉ tragedy
> for paper incke quilles & pindust.

Apparently a copy was also provided for the use of a distinguished guest. Thus at Trinity, 1670:

> for paper to writ out yᵉ Comedy for my Ld. Freschville.

Whether this custom prevailed a century earlier is doubtful. The 'both books' held by the Chancellor and High Steward[1] 'on the scaffold' at the performances of *Dido* in King's College Chapel in 1564, even if presented to these two officers by way of compliment[2], were, in Mr W. J. Lawrence's view, probably used as prompt-books. He writes to me:

> The stage being very broad, a prompter was required at either end. The players were not ordinary players and it was not derogatory to the Chancellor and the High Steward to prompt their own scholars.

Dr Boas points out that the B.M. MS. of *Sapientia Solomonis* was a copy made for Queen Elizabeth, and thinks it probable that copies were made for distinguished visitors for other than 'prompt' purposes. I agree with him.

Sometimes perhaps only the names of the dramatis personæ were given, which would explain the Trinity entry, 1554–5:

> for paper to write the names in owr Mrs shew

[1] Nichol's *Progresses of Q. Eliz.* I. 186 (ed. 1823).
[2] Boas, p. 93.

(possibly, but hardly probably, Christopherson's *Jephthes*).

DRESS OF THE ACTORS

It is needless to draw attention to the items in the accounts relating to the dress and the dressing of the actors—or to the lists of the players' garments preserved at Queens' College. An item in the King's accounts for 1554–5 has however an historical interest in connexion with the changes which followed the accession of Queen Mary:

Item sol. Carleton sacriste pro labore in conuertendis tunicis hystrionum in vestimenta ecclesie 20^d

We do not find however that even at King's theatrical performances were suspended during Mary's reign.

The stage-directions of Tomkis' Trinity play, *Lingua* (1607), prescribe the physical characteristics and dress of each of the dramatis personæ.

The actors' garments were kept from year to year in a chest (Trinity Accounts, 1562–3, 1663–4; Queens', 1547–8, 1640–1; Christ's, 1534–5) which stood at Queens' in the muniment room in the Tower, at Trinity (1664) in the Audit-Chamber. The chest at Queens' is still in existence.

For important occasions the royal wardrobe at the Tower could sometimes be drawn on, as is shown by the well known letter sent by the University to Lord Burleigh on 28th January, 1594/5:

There being in that Tragœdie sondry personages of greatest astate, to be represented in ancient princely attire[1].

[1] Cooper, *Ann.* II, 528.

MUSIC AT A PERFORMANCE

In 1669–70 Trinity College paid 2*s*. for '25 foot of quarters for ye Musick's Lattice.' This was for the Acting Chamber.

The music at a performance seems generally, as has been said, to have been provided by the waits of the town. But at Queens' on 1 March 1541, we have a payment of 12*d*. to one Tusher 'qui pulsabat organa in agendis comedijs.' And in the Trinity accounts for 1669–70 £2 is paid 'To ye University Musick for y^ir attendance 2 days at ye Comedy.' The dramatis personæ of *Senilis Amor* (1635/6) include 'Tibicines.'

LIGHTING OF THE STAGE

We have seen that at the performance of the plays in King's College Chapel before the Queen in 1564, the lighting was effected by torch-staves held by the guard. Many items in college accounts relate to the lighting of the stage. Thus:

Queens', 1522/3: 'pro cereis sive funeralibus que emimus propter comediam Plauti   3^s 5^d'
1540–1: 'pro candelabro,' 'pro 38 candelabris ex ferro.'
1541–2: 'pro..candelis..quum agebatur comœdia.'
1545–6, March 10: 'pro lucernis in Comœdia.'
1627–8: 'Torches for Comedie stage
             Candles 16^li Links 2 dozens for Comœdie.'
1633–4: ⎰'To the wax chaundler for 4 duz. of torches
         ⎱   1. 12. 0
          For 4 pound of wax lights   5. 8
          For the Comœdies.'
Trinity, 1546–7: 'for A great Rownd Candlesticke for the stage in the hall   4^s 6^d'

1547–48: 'for iij stone and a halfe of pyche 4ˢ 8ᵈ
for xxi frales for the cressets 23ᵈ
for pyche 16ᵈ
for torches the laste yere 4ˢ'
1549–50: 'for ij torches for yᵉ plaes in Christenmas 3ˢ'
1551–2: 'for ij lynckes for yᵉ showe on newyeres
day 20ᵈ'
1560–1: 'for 30 Irone candlestickes for the stage.. 5ˢ
for a greate nosell for yᵉ stage Lantehorne 8ᵈ'
1663–4: 'for candles, wax & tallow 1. 12. 1'
1664–5: 'for wax candles, Linkes & Torches 1. 14. 2'

The last line of the Epilogue of Walter Hawkesworth's *Labyrinthus* acted at Trinity 1602/3 is:

Acta esset hæc fabula lychni si abessent bene: si spectatores optime.

TIME AND LENGTH OF PERFORMANCE

The time of performance was probably as a rule the evening. The plays acted before Queen Elizabeth in King's College Chapel in 1564 lasted from about 9 p.m. to midnight, the lighting being effected by torch-staves carried by the guard.

On the other hand the performance of *Lælia* at Queens' in 1595 before the Earl of Essex and other lords took place 'after dinner,' 'the Day being turned into Nyght.'

The performance of Hacket's *Loiola* in the Hall of Trinity on 12 March 1622/3, began at 11. We are told that the hall was darkened and that the players had 'had order to abbreviate or contract' the play 'from six or seven hours to four or five' which the King 'sat out with good satisfaction'[1].

[1] Chamberlain's letter of March 21st.

On the other hand Prince Charles and the Elector Palatine were greatly bored by the length of Brooke's *Adelphe* on 4 March 1612/3. When *Adelphe* was played again on 1 May 1669 in the Trinity Comedy House before the Prince of Tuscany we hear that the performance 'lasted till about 9 at night.'

NAME OF THE PLAY OR OF THE SCENE DISPLAYED TO THE SPECTATORS

The title of the Comedy seems sometimes to have been fixed up on a wall. A speaker in the prologue to *Pastor Fidus*, acted at King's College *c.* 1590–1605, is made to say:

scena cognoscitur esse Arcadia: scylvam vides Erymanthi, Dianæ templum est ibi; comædiæ nomen parieti affixum vides: authorem scire, vel nescire, quid ad comœdiam.

On other occasions the name of the place where the events were supposed to occur was put up. The Trinity accounts for 1669 in connexion with the performance of *Adelphe* have the item: 'for painting NOLA upon ye stage. . 1ˢ 0ᵈ.' By this time possibly a change of scene took place in the course of the play. Hence the items in the Trinity accounts for 1664–5: 'For yᵉ Inscription of yᵉ 2 Scenes. . 1ˢ' and 1669–70: 'for. . writing 2 names.'

THE PROLOGUE

The earlier prologues, e.g. those of *Hymenæus* and *Victoria*, imitated the Prologues of Terence and gave a sketch of the situation and characters about to appear. Later prologues deal with wider topics. That of *Pastor Fidus* apologizes for the rawness of the actors who are to present it:

Prodeunt
actores noui, stulti fortasse, certè quidem adulescentuli
quorum nemo adhuc scenam attigit, alii[1] ne viderunt
   quidem.
Nemo septimu*m* in Academia complevit annum, aliqui
   ne annum quidem.

Moreover the mixed character of the play is something new and foreign. In the mouth of the objector,

Tragica hic comœdia pastoritia scilicet
Agenda est: primu*m* vnde genus hoc peregrinu*m*, et
   novu*m*
Deinde inter pastores tragicum. Res ipsa personis ne-
   quicquam convenit.

To this it is replied that Arcadian shepherds were not mere shepherds but great heroes and very remarkable men, and everything old was new once.

The Prologue-speaker further points out that we no longer turn to Comedies for moral examples and instruction:

ad comœdias non nisi
Delectationis et animi gratiâ accedimus.

The contrary doctrine is asserted in the prologue to W. Johnson's *Valetudinarium*, 1637/8:

poeta vester
Id studuit maximè ut mores corrigat, non ut risus excitet.
Sat laudis, mercedis satis sibi putabit fore
Si quis vestrum post peractam fabulam domum melior
   redierit
Et ad virtutes impensè magis animum adiunxerit.

[1] ? aliqui.

Adeste igitur æquo animo, agite animadvortite,
Nil moramur quam hilares, si secedatis boni.

The Prologue to *Lingua* (? 1602) similarly:

Our Muse describes no Louers passion
No wretched Father, ne vnthriftie Sonne
We are not wanton, or Satyricall
These haue their time and places fit, but we
Sad houres, and serious studies, to repriue
Haue taught seuere Philosophy to smile.

The prologue or epilogue often refers to the hostility
shown by Puritans to all theatrical performances.
Thus in the epilogue to *Clytophon*, the spectators are
admonished:

fauete vt fecistis histrionibus,
nolite artem comicam pati vestra negligentia
propter perpaucorum curiosam malitiam in nihilum
    recidere,
Honesta studiosorum oblectamenta promovete sedulo.

The whole of *Fucus* 1622/3 is an attack on the
Puritan attitude.

Before *The Birthe of Hercules* the 'Prologus
Laureatus' announces himself:

I am a Prologue; should I not tell you soe
You would scarse know me, 'tis soe longe agoe
Since Prologues were in use. Men put behinde
Now that they were wont to put before.
Thepilogue is in fashion, prologues no more.
But.. well befyttes a prologue an ould plaie...

And mark you that it is a Comedie,
Or tragicke Comedye, call yt which you will:
Tis no historie, Ballett, nor Boccas tale
No pleasant newe Interlude, no pretty toye:
No pestered deuise, wth Actors, crowded in
Drumbes, Ensignes, phiphes, targets & rusty swords.

Attempts are made to give some freshness of interest to the prologue in various ways.

The prologue to *Leander* as given for the second time in 1602/3 was spoken 'by Mr. Forrest' with a primrose which he addressed as

Terrestre sidus, hespere venientis anni

and compared to the play, and this prologue was borrowed for a later performance of *Pastor Fidus* (Trinity Coll. MS. R. 3. 37), where

Prologus præfert manu primulam.

Similarly the prologue of Vincent's *Paria* 1627/8 was delivered before King Charles by 'Mr Suckline' (Sir John Suckling)

Limacem in manu gerens & contrectans,

fondling a snail. Here too the snail is compared to the comedy.

The prologues of *Pastor Fidus* (*c.* 1590–1605), *The Returns from Parnassus* (*c.* 1599–1602), *Ignoramus* (1615), *Aristippus* (*c.* 1629/30), *The Rivall Friends* (1631/2) are in dialogue.

In the *Return from Parnassus II* the interlocutors are Boy [the proper Prologue-speaker], Stage-keeper, Momus and Defensor. The last is made to reflect on plays of a different type:

Frame[n] as well we might with easie straine
With far more praise and with as little paine
Storyes of loue, where forne the wondring bench
The lisping gallant might injoy his wench,
Or make some Sire acknowledge his lost sonne,
Found when the weary act is almost done.

For the prologue to *Aristippus* see under 'Plays and
Shows.'

Hausted's *Rivall Friends* acted and printed in 1632
was preceded by what was called 'The Introduction':

Being a Dialogue betwixt Venus, Thetis, and Phœbus,
sung by two Trebles, and a Base.

Venus (being Phosphorus as well as Vesper) appearing
at a window above as risen, calling to Sol, who lay in
Thetis lap at the East side of the stage, canoped with an
azure curtaine: at the first word that Venus sung, the
curtaine was drawne, and they discovered.

After the Dialogue was over, a Boy entered and
made a speech as on 'this Valentine's morning,'—
perhaps the date of the original performance—and
introduced the Prologue. The Prologue comes in
disguised as an old man. This was in reference to
'their Maiesties comming being deferr'd.'

Most sacred Majesties, if yee doe wonder
To be saluted by an *aged* Prologue,
Know that upon these *temples* I doe weare
An *Embleme* of our *Mothers fate*, who since
Shee has in expectation of your presence
Numbred the tedious moments, is growne *old*:
For each expecting minute that has pass'd
Has seem'd an *hower*, and every *hower* a *yeare*.
But will yee see what power yee retaine?
Wee by your presence are made young againe.
[He pulls off his head of haire and beard.

THE ARGUMENT

When the Prologue no longer gave the argument
of the play, it was followed sometimes by an 'Argu-
mentum.' That this was spoken is shown by the casts

of *Hispanus* (1596/7), where the argument was delivered by 'rec. Anderton jun.' (Anderton junior, freshman) and of *Paria*, 1627/8, where it was given by 'Mr Driwood.'

EPILOGUE

The Epilogus to *Lingua* has a dramatic character:

> Iudicious friends, it is so late at night,
> I cannot waken hungrie Appetite.
> . . . .

Vpon the *Plaudite* Appetitus awakes and runs in after Anamnestes.

PLAYS AND SHOWS

There were represented at Trinity in 1552–3 seven shows and one comedy, in 1560–1 four shows and three plays, at Christ's in 1563–4 a show and a play.

The distinction seems to have been a very definite one[1], but it is not easy to say what it was. In 1554/5 we hear at Trinity of 'our master's show.' The Master was then John Christopherson. If the show was his *Jephthes*, we are still more at a loss. At any rate this entry shows that a show was not always an irresponsible dramatic performance got up by students, and not by the official staff of the college.

The distinction perhaps lay in this—that 'a show' represented the mediæval tradition of a disguising,

[1] Yet cp. an item in the accounts of the Junior Bursar of Trinity in 1554–5 in regard to 'Sᵣ Vxenbridge playe and Syr Huttuns' where there is the marginal note 'charges of showes.'

and a play followed the form more or less of ancient tragedy or comedy. One might suppose that a 'show' was always in English. But this is doubtful. There was a show at King's after Queen Mary's accession on 'Anglia deformata & reformata,' which, we must presume from the title, was in Latin.

At Trinity shows as well as plays were produced by fellows and lecturers of the college.

The show probably relied for its success largely on its topical allusions, and satire: though such elements might enter into plays of regular form such as *Pedantius* and *Club Law*. Randolph in his prologue to his show *Aristippus* (printed 1630, and probably acted in 1629–30) makes much of the fact that he is now calling 'the show' again into life, after it had been forbidden for years on account of its licence in satire of individuals:

From Sloane MS 2531

The Scene: Cambridge

The Shewe being condemned for former abuses is raised vp by a Conjurer.

 Enter CONJURER *for a* Prologue:
Thou long dead
  Breake from thy marble prison, sleepe no more
  In drowsie darknes.
Enter SHEW *whipt vp by two furies*
       Are not my paines sufficient
  But ye must torture me wth the sad remembrance
  Of my desartes, sad causes of my exile?
Prol. Tis thy release I seeke, I come to file
  Those heavy shackles from thy wretched limbes
  And giue thee leaue to walke the stage againe

As free as Vertue Burne that wither'd Bayes
And wth fresh Laurell crowne thy sacred temples,
Cast off the maske of darknes & appeare
As glorious as thy sister Comedie
But first wth teares wash off thy guilty sinne:
Purge out those ill digested dregs of witt,
That vse their Inke to blott a spottles fame.
Let vs not haue particular men traduc'd
Whom private hate hath spurr'd thee to revile,
. . . .

Shew. Then from ye depth of Truth I here protest
I doe disclaime all petulant hate & malice.
     Ile not dare to say
That such a man paid for his ffellowshipp,
& had no Lerning, but in's purse. no officer
needs feare the sting of my detraction:
I giue all Leaue to fill their gutt*es* in quiett,
I make no dangerous Almanack*es*, no gull*es*,
No Post*es* wth biting newes, & envious packettes
You need not feare this shewe you that are bad
It is no parliam^t.

PLAYS IN ENGLISH

It is not very easy to understand the line taken by
the University or the Colleges with regard to plays
in English. *Gammer Gurton's Needle* was performed
at Christ's about 1554. The accounts of the Junior
Bursar of Trinity of 1559–60 include a payment of
8*s.* 10*d.* 'to Mr. Abithell for both the english plaies.'
Ezechias in English was acted before the Queen in
1564. But when the University was requested to
provide a comedy in English to be acted at Court at
Christmas 1592, great difficulties were raised.

The reply of the Vice-Chancellor and Heads ran:
having no practice in this Englishe vaine & beinge (as
wee think) nothing beseeminge our Students, specially

oute of the University, wee much doubt: and do find our principall actors (whom wee have of purpose called before us) very unwilling to playe in Englishe.

..Englishe Comedies, for that wee never used any, wee presentlie have none; to make or translate one in such shortnes of time wee shall not be able: and therefore, if wee must needes undertake the busines,...these two things wee would gladly desire: some further limitation of time for due preparation, and liberty to play in Latyn.

4 Dec. 1592.

Yet within a few years of this letter the scurrilous *Club Law* was acted at Clare Hall (*c.* 1599–1600) and the Parnassus trilogy at St John's about the same time. Phineas Fletcher's *Sicelides* and Tomkis' *Albumazar* were prepared for King James's visit in 1614/5, and later we have Hausted's *Rivall Friends* and Randolph's *Jealous Lovers* acted before King Charles and Queen Mary in 1631/2. And these are only a few cases out of many known to us.

And yet we note again a decree of Corpus Christi College of 1621/2 restricting English plays to the Christmas holidays and Candlemas Eve and Candlemas Day (modified a year later by including the day preceding Candlemas Eve).

REFRESHMENTS FOR SPECTATORS

Refreshments seem to have been provided for guests at the end of a performance. Cp. the epilogue to *Clytophon* (early 17th century?):

Verum abire tamen non sinam nisi prius biberitis,
Vos nunc valete obsecro,

and these items in the college accounts:

Queens', 1546–7: 'pro cervisia..quando agebantur comediæ   12ᵈ'
    1628–9: 'For beare spent at yᵉ comedies   1. 4. 9'
    St John's, 1594–5: 'to the poticary feb. 21. when the Doctors were invited to the house   37ˢ 8ᵈ'
    Trinity, 1598–9: 'for wyne at the Comodies   24ˢ 8ᵈ'
    1611–12: 'for burnt wyne & dyet bread at the entertaining of the Vice-Chancelloʳ and other strangers at the Commodies   45ˢ'
    1632: 'for Burnt wine at yᵉ Com̄edyes   £1. 12'
    1665: 'for wine spent at yᵉ comedies   £4. 6'
    1669: 'for Oranges spent upon yᵉ Prince & strangers at yᵉ two times of publick acting   14ˢ 4ᵈ'
    1670: 'For wine at yᵉ Comedy before yᵉ Duke of Ormond 12 qts of Canary 12 qts of Claret   £1. 18. 0
    For wine spent when it was acted before yᵉ University 8 qts of Canary and 6 qts of Claret £1. 3. 4, a pottle of Burnt claret 2ˢ 8ᵈ   [£1. 6. 0]
    To yᵉ Orangman for Oranges spent yᵉ 2 days of yᵉ Comedy upon yᵉ Spectators and actors   £2. 12. 0'

Similarly in 1671.

It was one of the duties of the stage-keepers to offer beer to the guests; see the prologue to *Returne from Pernassus II* where Momus says to the Stage-keeper:

You may doe better to busy youre selfe in prouiding beere, for the shew will be pittiful drie, pittifull drie.

SMOKING AT PLAYS

That smoking was not unknown in College halls at the performance of plays appears from a decree of the Vice-Chancellor and Heads in 1607 by which punishments were appointed for taking tobacco:

in any dining hall of colleges or at any other time and place of comedies or publick university tragedies shews or assemblies.   (Cooper, *Ann.* III, 28.)

REFRESHMENTS FOR THE ACTORS

The actors seem always to have been regaled as well as the guests. Thus in the Queens' College accounts:

1545–6: 'expendi in cibis pro actoribus.. comediæ 12^d'
1550–1: 'pro conviuio ludi...   11^s 8^d'

in those of Corpus:

1581–2: 'in largess to the Actors for a Beaver   20^d'

and in those of Trinity:

1549–50: 'for puddinges for Mr Atkingson players 8^d
for Chesse for Mr Atkingesons players   7^d
for good aile . . . for Mr Atkinsons play   6^d'
1550–1: 'for ii Loynes & a breste of mutton for
Mr Atkynsons players   [deest]'
1558–9: 'geuen vnto Sr Shackelocke & Sr Redman
for a breakfast for ye players in their shewe   2^s'
1559–60: 'to the bachelars breakfast for there
tragedye   2^s'
1568–9: 'to Mr Redman for his players breakefast 2^s'
1598–9: 'to the Actors to make a supper   53^s 4^d'
1662: 'To the Actors for a supper   1. 12. 2'
1669: 'to ye Tapster at ye Sun for bear, pipes & bread
& buttyr had by ye Actors   2. 8. 0
for Tobacco taken by ye Actors   11. 3'
1670: 'For wine at ye Comedy before ye Duke of
Ormond 6 qts of Canary and 6 qts of Claret for y^e
Actors   19^s
for Tobacco & Pipes for ye Actors   13^s 4^d'
1671: 'for ye Actors 7 quarts of Canary & 12 . . claret
                                                1. 7. 2
For wine for ye Actors spent at ye Comedy præpared
for ye prince of Orange 10 qu^{ts} of canary & 10 quarts
of claret   1. 10. 0
to Mrs Powell for beare for ye Actors   13. 0
To Dr Wrag for ye Actors tobacco   9. 6'

In these last years at Trinity the actors seem to have been also presented with gloves:

1670: 'To Mr Moody for Kid Gloves for 19 Actors
...at 2^s ye paire   [1. 18. 0]'
  1671: 'for gloves for ye Actors   2. 14. 4'

RIOTING AT THE TIME OF PLAYS AND PRECAUTIONS AGAINST IT

The performance of a play seems to have drawn great numbers of people to the college, and those who were not admitted seem to have vented their feelings by breaking the windows. Many items in the accounts relate to the mending of broken glass after a performance or to the precautions taken to prevent such damage. Thus:

Queens', 1547, 23º februarij: 'solui vitriario pro vitro quod frangebatur quando agebantur comediæ in Aula 8^s'
  1551–2: 'vitriario pro reparatione 40 pedum vitri in occidentali fenestra aulæ post lusus   8^s 4^d'
  1594–5: 'for repairing th' hall windowes after the plaies   45^s'
Trinity, 1560–1: 'for glasinge a windowe in Mr Vice M^r his chamber and for mendinge his windowes broken at ye stage playes   9^s 1^d'
  1578–9: 'for thyrtye foote of new glasse after the playes, in the hall windowes   15^s'
  1582–3: 'for lv foot of newe glasse in the hall after the playes   28^s'
King's, 1561–2: 'pro reparatione vitrarum fenestr. in Aula   16^d'
  1606–7: 'pro reparacione variarum fenestrarum tam in Cubiculo Sociorum quam in Aula communi et parlura fractarum tempore le Englyshe Commodies   4^s 10^d'
St John's, 1568–9: 'allowed Sr Mead towardes the glaysinge of his windowes wch were broken dowen at the plaies   5^s'
Caius, 1616: 'to..the glasyer for mending the hall windowes broken at the Comedie...'

To provide against such damage, the windows seem either to have been protected by netting, or taken down altogether: while a careful watch was kept for mischief-makers.

St John's, 1578–9 (before the performance of *Richardus Tertius*): 'for nettes to hange before the windowes of ye Halle   6^s'

1585–6: 'To the glacer for taking downe and setting vpp the windowes   20^s'

1597–8: 'To ye Glasier...for taking downe & setting vp the glasse in the hall windowes...& for sixteen quarrelles of glasse after the Comedie feb. 16   44^s 4^d'

Trinity, 1567–8: 'for Taiken downe and setting vpp againe of xxii paines of Glass in th' hall at ye playes 3^s 4^d'

1568–9: 'Arthure glasier for takinge downe the glasse in the sex lower windowes of the hall and repayrenge them before the plaies   6^s 8^d'

1572–3: 'For takinge downe and repairinge off xxxix paines off glasse at the plaies   39^s'

1586–7: 'for taking downe and setting vp the glasse wyndowes at the last playes   13^s 4^d'

1598–9: 'geven to those that watched ye glasse windowes one the Comodie night...   6^s'

1664–5: 'For watching and defending ye walls   6^d'

As a further security for an orderly performance, a number of students were appointed 'Stage-keepers' or, as we should say, Stewards. They wore smart dress, sometimes a visor or steel cap, and carried links to guide the guests of the college across the dark court. The story of the misbehaviour of one Punter late scholar of St John's in the early part of 1578/9 told in a letter of the Vice-Chancellor John Hatcher of 9th Dec. 1579 [1] gives a lively picture of

---

[1] *Domestic Papers, Elizabeth*, vol. 38, 1.

the disorders of a play-night. Punter (whom we
know as one of the actors in *Hymenæus*):

> vncased (as they call it) one of the stagekeepers of Caius
> colledge pluckinge of his visor; and at the first playes..
> at Trinitie Colledge had violently pressed to come into
> yᵉ colledge, euen against yᵉ wills of such Maysters of
> Arts as were there appointed to see good order kept,
> insomuch that he had almost set that house and S. Johns
> together by yᵉ eares; and afterwards to reuenge himselfe
> for yᵉ repulse there sustained had priuely crept into
> Benet [Corpus Christi] Colledge, & takinge vpon him
> yᵉ habit of a stage keper there, to yᵉ greate disturbaunce
> of the whole assembly, did assault one of Trinitie colledge,
> whom also he afterward chalengid into the feilds.

In the dialogue-prologue to *The Returne from
Pernassus II* (? 1602–3) Momus is made to say:

> The Pilgrimage to Pernassus and the returne from
> Pernassus haue stood the honest Stage keepers in many
> a Crownes expence for linckes and vizards: purchased
> [many] a Sophister a knock [with] a clubbe: hindred
> the buttlers box[1], and emptied the Colledge barrells.

On 20 Feb. 1606/7 at the time of a comedy at
King's College, 'the hall being full not only of the
inferior sort, but also of divers young noblemen,
doctors, bachelors in divinity and masters of arts,'
the windows were broken by stones cast by scholars
and others with loud outcries for two hours together[2].

A still more famous riot was that which occurred
between the gates of Trinity and St John's early in
February 1609/10. All the documents as preserved
in the *Acta Curiae* of the University were published

---

[1] Was the 'buttlers box' a collecting box for the poor?
[2] Cooper, *Ann.* III, 24.

in 1906 by the late Registrary, Mr J. W. Clark, in a pamphlet called *The Riot at the Great Gate of Trinity*[1].

Here we have allegations of stage-keepers, some of whom were Masters of Arts and Fellows of Trinity, using links and clubs as weapons of offence against the Johnians whom they wished to keep out, of stones thrown from the Gateway Tower, and of a rush by Johnians armed with clubs which drove the stage-keepers within their own gates. The dress of different stage-keepers is here described:

'a stagekeeper apparrelled in a light colour suyte of saye with lace of ye same colour,' 'a stagekeeper in a whyte suyte guarded with red lace having a headpeace on his head,' 'a stagekeeper wearing a redd suyte laced downwards with whyte and a capp of harnes,' 'a stagekeeper..in a whyte fryse jerkin..with a dager and sworde drawne,' 'a stagekeeper yt wore a green suyte with puffes,' 'a stagekeeper in a rugg gowne and a steele cap.'

Only very late do we get a hint that admission to plays was regulated by the institution of tickets. The Trinity accounts for 1664–5 have the entry:

'For wax to make Ticketts   4^d'

[1] Cambridge Antiquarian Society Octavo Publications, No. XLIII.

CHRONOLOGICAL TABLE OF PERFORMANCES OF COLLEGE PLAYS AT CAMBRIDGE

M S

CHRONOLOGICAL TABLE

Year	Date	College	Play	Source
1482	Christmas-day	King's	'ludos'	Mundum Book
1482/3	Jan. 1	King's	'lusoribus'	Mundum Book
1484/5	Feb. 2	King's	'le disgysyns'	*Liber Communarum*
1489	Dec. 31	King's	'le disgysynges'	Mundum Book
1496	Christmas	King's	'ludos'	Mundum Book
1508/9	Jan. 14	King's	'lusu'	Mundum Book
1510	Christmas	King's	'lusu'	Mundum Book
1510–11	Xmas or New Year	King's Hall	'comedia Terentij in Ludo'	Accounts
1516–17	Xmas or New Year	King's Hall	'pro ludo..therencij'	Accounts
1520–32		St John's	T. Artour's *Microcosmus* and *Mundus Plumbeus*	Bale, *Cent.* IX, 16
1522/23		Queens'	'comedia Plauti'	Magnum Journale
1531/2	? Feb.	Christ's	'ye play'	Coll. acc.
1532/3	Ash Wednesday	Christ's	'ye play'	Coll. acc.
1533	Christmas?	Christ's	'ij plays'	Coll. acc.
1534–35		Christ's	'the plays' ('to Mr Townley')	Coll. acc.

1535	Christmas	King's	'ludorum'	Mundum Book
1535–44		St John's	T. Watson's *Absalon*	Ascham's *Scholemaster*, ed. Mayor, p. 169
1536	Christmas	King's	'ludorum'	Mundum Book
		St John's	Aristophanes' *Plutus* (in Greek)	Mullinger, *Hist.* II, 73
1537–38	Christmas	Christ's	'the tragedy,'	Coll. acc.
1539	Feb.	Christ's	'playes' ('Mr Cawthorn')	Coll. acc.
1540/1		Queens'	'pro comedijs'	Magn. Journ.
1541–42	Christmas or later	King's	'ludorum'	Mundum Book
1541/2	Feb.	Queens'	'comœdia'	Magn. Journ.
1542/3	Jan. or Feb.	Queens'	R. Textor's *Thersites* ('actio dialogi textoris' 'miles gloriosus in comœdia')	Magn. Journ.
1544	Christmas	King's	'ludi natalis'	Mundum Book
1544/5	March	Christ's	*Pammachius*	Cooper, *Ann.* I, 422
1545	Christmas	King's	'ludos natalicios'	Mundum Book
1545/6	Feb.	Queens'	'comœdijs magistrorum Perne et Yale' *Lælia* perhaps Perne's play. But see under 1547	{Magn. Journ. {Miscell. A, fo. 46b

Date	Time	College	Play	Source
1546–47		Christ's	'the play' (Mr Pierpoynte)	Coll. acc.
1546–47		Trinity	'the stage in the hall,' 'the playes' (Sr Burton)	Sen. Burs. acc.
			? Aristophanes' *Pax* in Greek	J. Dee (see *D.N.B.*)
1547	Jan. or Feb.	Queens'	'comedias' ('Mr Yale') ? *Lelia*	{ Magn. Journ. / Miscell. A, fo. 46b }
1547	Christmas	Christ's	'a play'	Coll. acc.
1547–48		Trinity	'plaing gere' (Mr Donnell)	Sen. Burs. acc.
1547–48	Jan.	Queens'	*Persa* (? Mr Gastoyn)	Magn. Journ.
	Jan. or Feb.	Queens'	*Adelphe, Heli* (? Dˢ Herrison)	
1548	Christmas	King's	'ludorum'	Mundum Book
1548/9	Feb. or March	Queens'	*Penulus* (Mr Yale) *hypocrisis* (tragœdia) (The President & Mr gascoyn)	Magn. Journ.
1548–49	Christmas	Christ's	'ye players'	Coll. acc.
1549		Trinity	'Mr Thulace play'	Stew. acc.
1549–50	(before Jan. 21)	Queens'	'comedia'.. (Mr Reymond)	Magn. Journ.
1550–51		Corpus	'ye playe'	Coll. acc.

1550–51	Christmas and New Year	Trinity	'Mr Cocroste plaie' 'Mr Atkinsons play', 'Stilles play'	Stew. acc. 1549–50
			'Mr Nevysons players', 'Mr Thulace players', 'Mr Atkynsons players', 'ludus' (Mr Barnarde)	Stew. acc. 1550–51
1550–51	Christmas or Jan.	Queens'	'ludus' (Ds Robinson)	Magn. Journ.
		Queens'	'comedia' (Mr Barnarde)	Magn. Journ.
	March		'comedia' (Ds Iosslyne)	Magn. Journ.
1550–51		Christ's	'Sir Stephenson..his play',	Coll. acc.
1551–52		Christ's	'S. Stephenson play' [perhaps the two items deal with a single performance at Xmas 1551]	Coll. acc.
1551–52		Trinity	'Mr Godsalfe..his playe'	Jun. Burs. acc.
			'Mr Malham..*Troas*',	Jun. Burs. acc.
			'Mr Rudde..*Menechmus*'	Jun. Burs. acc.
			'Sr Allington..ye showe'	Sen. Burs. acc.
1551–52		Queens'	'lusus..D. Josselyn'	Magn. Journ.
			'lusus..D. Maye'	Magn. Journ.

1551–52		Queens'	'posterior lusus D. Josselyn (tragedia)'	Magn. Journ.
1552–53	(before 16 Jan.)	King's	'ludorum per duas noctes'	Mundum Book
1552–53		Queens'	'Mro Robynson..comœdia'	Magn. Journ.
1552–53		Christ's	'Mro Thorpe..tragœdia'	Magn. Journ.
			'Sir Stephenson..his plaies'	Coll. acc.
1553	Christmas	Trinity	'yᵉ tragedie'	Coll. acc.
			'Sʳ Wendon..hys shew'	
			'Sʳ Ederrington..hys shew'	
			'Mʳ Raynolds..hys Comedye'	
			'Sʳ Uxenbrydge..hys shew'	
			'Sʳ Newton..hys shew'	Jun. Burs. and Stew. acc.
			'yᵉ shew cawled *Anglia Deformata & Anglia Restituta*'	
			'Sʳ Hutton..hys shew'	
			'Sʳ Style..hys shew'	

1553	Christmas	Christ's	'Mr Stephenson..his plaie' 'Mr Persevall..at ye latten plaie'	Coll. acc.
1553–54		Queens'	'Mri Mey..tragœdia' 'Mri Robinson.. comœdia *Stichus*'	Magn. Journ.
1554–55		Christ's	'ye play'	Coll. acc.
		Trinity	'Sr Uxenbridge playe' 'Sr Huttuns *de crumena perdita*' 'of Mr..hys shew'	Jun. Bur. acc.
1555	Christmas	King's	'ludorum'	Mundum Book
1555–56		Christ's	'iij playes and a shewe'	Coll. acc.
1555–56		St John's	'Mr Tailer..ye dialogue'	Coll. acc.
1556–57		St John's	'Mr Lakyn his playe'	Coll. acc.
1557	Jan. 1	Trinity	'showe' 'Mr Oxenbridg..players'	Jun. Burs. acc.
1557	Jan. 7	Trinity	'a commedye of Plautus'	Cooper, II, 111, 112
1557–58		Trinity	'Sr Hawes & Sr Longe.. shewes' 'Sr Shackelocke..players'	Stew. acc.

1558–59	Trinity	'Sr Shackelocke & Sr Redman..shewe'	Stew. acc.
		'Mr Mettam..players'	Stew. acc.
		'Sr Legg & Sr West..players'	Stew. acc.
1559–60	Christ's	'Sr Lacocke..players'	Stew. acc.
		'Sr Chattertonnes play'	Coll. acc.
1559–60	St John's	'Mr Stevensonnes play the playe'	Coll. acc.
1559–60	Trinity	'Sr Layeoke..showe'	
		'Sr Redmaine..*Hecuba*'	
		'the bachelars..tragidye'	
		'Mr Oxenbridge..tragidye—*Oedipus*'	Stew. acc. and Jun. Burs. acc.
		'Mr Beamond..comedye'	
		'Mr Hawes..playe—*Mostellaria*'	
		'Mr Abithell..both the english plaies'	
		'Mr Penny..*Sapientia Solomonis*'	

1560–61	Jan.	Trinity	'Mr Penny..shewe' 'MrNewtone..*Amphytrio*' 'Mr Hudsone..*Troas*' 'Mr Legge..*Medea*' 'Mr Barrete..*Acolastus*' 'Mr Abythell for Sr Per-kinsone his shewe (and) Lewes shewe' 'Sr Valinger..shewes' 'Brittan..shew'	Jun. Burs. acc. and Stew. acc.
1561		Queens'	'spectaculum'	Magn. Journ.
1561–62		King's	'ludicrorum'	Mundum Book
1561–62		St John's	'ye stage plaies'	Coll. acc.
1561–62		Christ's	'Mr Chatherton's playe'	Coll. acc.
1561–62		Trinity	'v playes'	Stew. acc.
1561–62		Queens'	'Dño Rastall..comedia' 'Mro Igulden..comedia'	Magn. Journ.
1561–62		Jesus	'the playes'	Coll. acc.
1562–63		Jesus	'*Adelphe, Curculio*'	Coll. acc.
1562–63		Trinity	'Mr Shaclocke..*Pseudolus*' 'Mr Chapman & Parkyn-son..*John babtiste*'	Jun. Burs. acc.

1562–63	Trinity	'Mr Browne & D. Wilkynson.. *Christus Triumphans*'	Jun. Burs. acc.
		'Mr Legge & Bingam.. *Adelphus*'	
		'Mr Wallei.. *Phormio*'	
		[In the Steward's acc. 'Mr Ruds playe' seems to refer to the last above]	
1562–63 (not later than Feb.)	Queens'	'D. Rockerye.. comœdia'	Magn. Journ.
		'D. Linforde.. comœdia'	
		'D. Som.. comœdia'	
		'Mr Igulden.. comœdia'	
1563–64 (not later than Feb.)	Jesus	'*Eunucus*'	Coll. acc.
1563–64	Queens'	'Mr Lynforde.. comœdia'	Magn. Journ.
1563–64	Christ's	'a shoe and a playe'	Coll. acc.
1563–64	St John's	'playes'	Coll. acc.
		'Mr Cartwright.. *Trinummus*'	
1563–64	Trinity	'Mr Legg & Mr Foorde.. the seconde playe'	Jun. Burs. acc.
		'Mr Browne & Coke.. *Bachides*'	

1564	Aug. 6	King's	'Mr Parkynson & Powell'	Jun. Burs. acc.
	" 7	King's	'Mr Wilkinson..his playe' *Aularia* (by University) E. Halliwell's *Dido* (by King's College)	Stew. acc. Cooper, *Ann.* II, 193–202
	" 8	King's	N. Udall's *Ezechias* (in English) (by King's Coll.)	
	" 9	King's	Sophocles' *Ajax Flagellifer* (in Latin) (by King's Coll.)	
	" 10	Hinchin-brook	'The *imprisoned bishops*.. a show'. (by Cambridge students)	Boas, p. 382
1564 1564–65	Christmas	Jesus Trinity	'the dialogge and shewe' 'Mr Legge & Mr Powel.. *Stichus*' 'Mr Wilkinson & Mr Cooke..playe' 'Mr Gybson and Mr Davyd..*Philamira*' 'Sr Redmayn..showe'	Coll. acc. Jun. Burs. acc.

Date		College		Authority
1564–65	(not later than Jan.)	Queens'	'Mr Tower..comedia'	Magn. Journ.
1565–66		Trinity	'Mr Browne..*Asotus*'	Jun. Burs. acc.
			'Mr Legge & Mr Gibson.. *Asinaria*'	
			'Mr Powell and Mr Dun- nynge..*Crumenaria*'	
1566–67		Trinity	'Mr Gillpen & Mr Byll.. *Menechmus*'	Jun. Burs. acc.
1567–68		Christ's	'Mr Legge..*Jephthes*'	Coll. acc.
			'Writes showe at Christ- [mas]'	
1567–68		Jesus	'ye plaie',	Coll. acc.
			'or playes',	Coll. acc.
1567–68		Trinity	'Mr Forthes shewe'	Jun. Burs. acc. and Stew. acc.
			'Mr Reedman (Redman) & Mr Stannopp..play',	
			'Mr Aldridg & Mr Wilks playes'	
1568		Peterhouse	[..play'	*Accounts of St Mary the Great*, ed. Foster, [p. 167
1568/9	? Jan.	St John's	'Sr Hayt & Sr Ellis..the shewe in the gallery'	Coll. acc.
	? Feb.		'the plaies'	Coll. acc.

1568–69		Jesus	'Mr Day & Wod..the playes in the chappell'	Coll. acc.
1568–69	(end of Jan.?)	Trinity	'Mr Redman..playe' 'Mrs Stanhope and Doddinge..play'	Jun. Burs. acc. and Stew. acc.
1569–70		Trinity	'Sr Bedwell & Sr Ashburne..playe'	Jun. Burs. acc.
? 1570–75		Trinity Hall	*Herodes*	Dedication
1570–71		Trinity	'the playes' (Mr Gibson, Mr Gilpin, Mr Wilkes, Mr Stanhop, Mr Dod-dinge, Messrs Cosen and Bennet)	Jun. Burs. acc.
1571–72		Peterhouse	'comœdia' 'in aula'	Computus Roll.
1572–73		Trinity	'plaies' (Mr Farrand)	Jun. Burs. acc.
1573–74		Trinity	'the playes'	Jun. Burs. acc.
1573/4	Jan. or Feb.	Queens'	'the playe'	Magn. Journ.
1575–76	March or Ap.	Peterhouse	'the comedie'	Magn. Journ.
1575–76		Queens'	'ludos'	Comp. Roll.
1575/6	(not after Jan.)	St John's	'the Scollers..playe'	Magn. Journ.
1576–77		Corpus	'the playe' (Mr Duffield) 'the Comœdye'	Coll. acc. Coll. acc.

1577	Christmas	Jesus	'Mr Wilshawe..ye comedie'	Coll. acc.
1578	July		a comedy rehearsed for performance at Audley End	Boas, p. 111
1578-79		Trinity	'playes'	Jun. Burs. acc.
		Caius	'stagekeepers'	*S.P.Dom.Eliz.*vol. 38,1
1578-79		Corpus	'[Mr Nicholls]..ye comedyes'	Coll. acc.
1578-9	Bachelor's commencement	St John's	'Mr Stringer..ye tragedy' (*Legge's Richardus III*) 'the playes' (? *Hymenæus*)	Coll. acc.
1579	Christmas Eve	Jesus	'Mr Wilsha..*Bacchides*'	Coll. acc.
1579	Christmas	St John's	'the playe' (*Victoria?*)	Coll. acc.
1580 (or 1586)		Peterhouse	*Duns Furens*	Nashe, *Works*, ed. McKerrow, III, 80
1580/1	6 Feb.	Trinity	'the playes' (*Pedantius?*)	Jun. Burs. acc.
1581-82		Corpus	'the Comædie'	Coll. acc.
1581-82		Jesus	'Mr Murgetrod..*puer vapulans*'	Coll. acc.
1581/2	5 March	(? at Cambridge)	*Solymannidæ*	Date on MS.

Date	Occasion	College	Title	Reference
1582		St John's	'the Comedy'	Coll. acc.
1582–83	? Christmas	Trinity	'the playes'	Jun. Burs. acc.
1582/3	17 March	St John's	'the tragedy' (*Richardus III?*)	Coll. acc.; Tanner MS. 306
1582/3	Feb.	Pembroke	'comœdia quam ipse [Ds T. Mudde] composuit' (satire on the Mayor of Cambridge, probably in English)	Cooper, *Annals*, v. 314 and MS. Baker III, 427.
1582/3	Feb.	Corpus	'scenici ludi'	Coll. archives
1583	Christmas	St John's	'*Persa* in Plautus'	Coll. acc.
c. 1583			J. Watson's (Sophocles') *Antigone* (in Latin), publ. 1581	G. Harvey, *Marginalia*
1583	Dec.	Trinity	'Mr Palmer & Mr Farrand ...theire Comœdeys'	Jun. Burs. acc.
1585–86	Dec. or Jan.	St John's	[Windows taken down]	Coll. acc.
1585/6	? March	St John's	'the playes' (Nashe's *Terminus et non terminus?*)	Coll. acc.
1585/6 (?)		Peterhouse	*Duns Furens*	Nashe, III, 80
		Clare Hall	*Tarrarantantara*	

Date	College	Play	Source
1586/7	Trinity	'the playes,' 'the last playes' (? *Richardus Tertius*)	Jun. Burs. acc. MS.
1588/9	Queens'	'corde for the stage' [? *Miles Gloriosus*]	Mag. Journ. Thos. Ball, *Life of John Preston* in Clarke's *Lives*, 1677
1589–90	Trinity	'Mr Milner..comedies'	Sen. Burs. acc.
1590–91	Trinity	'the Comedie in Christmas'	Jun. Burs. acc.
		'a comedie..Mr Thomson, (ditto) Mr Boulton'	Sen. Burs. acc.
1590–1605	King's	*Pastor Fidus*	Coll. acc.
1591–92	Christ's	*Troilus* (if a play)	Magn. Journ.
1591/2	Queens'	'Mr Meriton..yᵉ Comedie' [? *Miles Gloriosus*]	J. H. Gray, *Hist. of Queens' Coll.* p. 135
c. 1592	Trinity	Alabaster's *Roxana*	Mundum Book
1592/3	King's	'comedia'	Magn. Journ. 1593–4
1592/3	Queens'	'the comodie'	Sen. Burs. acc.
1594/5	Trinity	'the playes' (Mr Sledd) (two comedies and a tragedy—Cooper, II, 529)	

Year	Date	College	Play	Authority
1594–95	c. 28 Feb.	King's	'the Comedies'	Mundum Book. (See Cooper, II, 539)
1594–95		Queens'	'a Comedy' (*Lælia*)	Add. MS. 5852
1594–95	? 21 Feb.	St John's	'the plaies'	Coll. acc.
1595–96		Jesus	'the show'	Coll. acc.
1595–96		Corpus	'Robinsons showe'	Coll. acc.
1596/7	13 Jan.	St John's	'Dno Robinson..com[edia?]'	Coll. acc.
1596/7	Jan. or Feb.	Corpus	*Silvanus*	Douce MS. 234
1596/7	March?	St John's	'Sr Butts..comedy'	Coll. acc.
1597	Dec. 9	St John's	*Hispanus*	Douce MS. 234
1597/8	Feb. 16	St John's	*Machiavellus*	Douce MS. 234
1598	Christmas	Jesus	'the Comedie' (? *Silvanus*)	Coll. acc.
1598–99		Trinity	'ye comodye'	Coll. acc.
			'the Comodie nightes' (? *Leander*)	Jun. Burs. Acc.
1598–99		King's	'Comedia'	Mundum Book
?1598–99		St John's	*Pilgrimage to Parnassus*	
1599–1600		Clare Hall	*Club Law*	
? c. 1600		Christ's (if by R. Bernard)	*The Birthe of Hercules*	Internal evidence, and Fuller MS. Jesus Coll.
?1600–1601		St John's	*Return from Parnassus I*	

				Internal evidence
? 1602		Trinity	*Lingua*	
? 1602–3		St John's	*Return from Parnassus II*	
1602/3	Com. Bacch. Feb. or March	Trinity	*Leander*	Date on MSS.
? 1604–5		Trinity	*Labyrinthus*	Tanner MS. 306, cast
1605	Christmas	St John's	*Locus, Corpus, Motus, etc.*	Coll. acc.
			'a Comedie',	Cast in Emm. MS.
1606/7	20 Feb.	King's	? *Zelotypus*	Mundum Book
			'Dno Fletcher..le englishe	Cooper, *Ann.* III, 24
			Comodye'	J. H. Gray, *Hist. of*
1607		Queens'	'the plaies'	*Queens' Coll.* p. 133
1608–9		Trinity	'the Commodies'	Sen. Burs. acc.
			Andrea	Stew. acc.
1609–10		Trinity	'the Commodie'	Stew. acc.
1611–12	? Xmas Feb.	Trinity	'the Commodies'	Stew. acc.
			S. Brooke's *Adelphe*	Trin. Coll. MS. R.
				3.9
1612/3	3 March	Trinity	*Scyros*	MSS.
	4 March	Trinity	*Adelphe*	MSS.
1613	Dec. 'the audite'	Trinity	'the Batchelors..a Commedy'	Sen. Burs. acc.
	Christmas	Corpus	'a comedie'	Coll. acc.
1613/4	Feb.	Jesus	'ye stage'	Coll. acc.

1613-14	24 March	Trinity	'the Schollers Commedie' *Scyros*	Sen. Burs. acc. C.U.L. MS. Ee. v. 16, gives date '1613'
? 1614-15		? Trinity	*Band, Cuffe and Ruffe*	Ent. Stat. Reg. 10 Feb. 1614/5
		? Trinity	*Worke for Cutlers*	Ent. Stat. Reg. 4 July, 1615
1614/5	March 7	Trinity	Cecill's *Æmilia* (St John's play)	Cooper, *Ann.* III, 70 and Sen. Burs. acc.
	March 8	Trinity	Ruggle's *Ignoramus* (Clare play)	
	March 9	Trinity	Tomkis' *Albumazar*	
	March 10	Trinity	Brooke's *Melanthe*	
	March 11	King's	Fletcher's *Sicelides*	
	May 13	Trinity	*Ignoramus* (Clare)	
1615	Dec.	Trinity	'the Audit Comedy'	Sen. Burs. acc.
1615	2 Feb.	Trinity	'the Shewe'	Sen. Burs. acc.
1615/6	'week before Shrovetide'	Trinity	'the Shewe'	Sen. Burs. acc.
1615/6	12 March	? Royston	'the comedy to be acted at Court' (Trinity) *Susenbrotus*	Cooper, *Ann.* III, 102

Date	Detail	College	Play	Authority
1615/6		Caius	'the Comedie'	Coll. acc.
? 1616		Trinity	Euribates?	
? 1616		Sidney Sussex	Lingua	
1617		Trinity	May's *Julius Cæsar*	Internal evidence
1618	Christmas	St John's	*Pathomachia* (if acted)	Cooper,V,355; D'Ewes, *College Life*², p. 61
			Stoicus Vapulans	
1618–27		Jesus	*Adrastus parentans*	MS.
1618/9	10 Feb.	Trinity	*Fraus Honesta*	Trin. Coll. MS. 995
				Mod. Lang. Rev. II,152
				Halliwell's *Dic.*
? 1620/1		Corpus	*Sophomorus*	'Acta capituli' C.C.C.
1621/2			'in ludo scenico Dⁿⁱ Hull' [apparently in English]	
			'in ludo scenico Dⁿⁱ Brodrib'	
1622–23	Feb. 28 and March 12	Jesus	'yᵉ comodie'	Coll. acc.
1622/3		Trinity	*Loiola*	
			Labyrinthus	Printed book
1622/3	(? away from Cambridge)	Queens' and at Newmarket	*Fucus Histriomastix*	See edition, 1909

Year	Date	College / Place	Plays	MS.
1624	Dec.	King at Cambridge	? plays	
? c. 1625		Emmanuel	*Pseudomagia*	
? c. 1625			*Cancer*	
c. 1626–31		Trinity	Randolph's *Aristippus, Conceited Pedlar, The Entertainment (Muses Looking-Glasse), Hey for Honesty, Cornelianum Dolium*	
1626/7		D. of Buckingham at Cambridge	? plays	
1627/8		Queens'	'the comedie'	Coll. acc. See Searle's *Hist. of Queens'*, Part II, p. 458
1627/8	3 March	Trinity	*Paria*	Emm. MS. 1.3.16, etc.
1628/9		Queens'	'ye comedies'	Coll. acc.
1629	24 Sept.	Trinity	? *Senile Odium* / *Fraus Honesta*	Cooper, III, 219; Stew. acc.
1631/2	March 22	Trinity	'ye Commedyes' / *The Jealous Lovers*	Cooper, III, 250

		? King's		King's Coll. acc.
1631/2			'Comœdiarum ad ad-ventum Regis' [perhaps those given at Trinity?]	
1631/2	19 March	Queens'	*Versipellis*	Cast
		Queens' or at Newmarket?	*Rivall Friends*	
? c. 1633		Jesus	J. Rickets' *Byrsa Basilica*	Internal evidence
1633–4		Queens'	'the comedies'	Archives No. 25
? c. 1634		? St John's	T. Sparrowe's *Confessor*	
1635/6	c. Feb. 4 or 5	[Queens'?]	[Hausted's] *Semilis Amor*	Dated '1635' on MS.
1637–38	? at Christmas	Corpus	'the stage in the hall'	Audits [Rawl. Poet. 9
1637/8	Feb. 6	Queens'	*Valetudinarium*	Emn. MS.
				Archives No. 27
1638	July	Corpus	'ye comedye'	Audits
1638/9	2 Feb.	Trinity	'the stage at the upper end'	Printed book
1639/40		Trinity	*Naufragium Joculare*	Sen. Burs. acc.
1641/2	March 12, Saturday	Trinity	'Sr Nicols his comedy'	Coll. acc.
			'Ds Cooleys Comedy'	Cooper, III, 321
			The Guardian	Sen. Burs. acc.
1661/2	Feb. or March	Trinity	'two Comœdyes'	Jun. Burs. acc.
			'ye Latine Comedie'	Epilogue *to Adelphe*
			[Apparently *The Silent Woman* and *Adelphe*]	

1662/3	Jan. March 16	Trinity	'two Comedies' 'comedie before yᵉ Duke of Monmouth'	Jun. Burs. acc.
1663–64		Trinity	'yᵉ Comedie'	Jun. Burs. acc.
1664–65		Trinity	'yᵉ 2 Comedies'	Jun. Burs. acc.
1668–69		Trinity	'yᵉ comedy' *Adelphe* (performed 3 times, twice 'publicly'—before D. of Tuscany on May 1)	Jun. Burs. acc.
1669–70		Trinity	'a comedy' (performed once before the University and once before the Duke of Ormond), (c. April 21)	Jun. Burs. acc.
1670	c. Nov.	Trinity	'yᵉ comedy acted before yᵉ University' 'yᵉ comedy prepared for yᵉ Prince of Orange' (i.e. for Nov. 26)	Jun. Burs. acc.
1675	June 28		Joshua Barnes, *The Academie or The Cambridge Dunns*	Emm. Coll. MS. III. 1. 4.

1676	June 26		Joshua Barnes, *The Academic* or *The Cambridge Dunns*	Emm. Coll. MS. III. 1. 4
1683	? acted		Joshua Barnes, *Landgartha*	Emm. Coll. MS. III. 1. 2
1693	? acted		Joshua Barnes (imitation of Plautus' *Trinummus*)	Emm. Coll. MS. III. 1. 2
	? acted		Joshua Barnes, *Englebert*	Emm. Coll. MS. III. 1. 2
1745–47		Pembroke	*A Trip to Cambridge, or The Grateful Fair*	*Poems* of C. Smart, 1791
c. 1835			"It is only three years since an English play was acted in one of the halls with the sanction of the Master of the College and the Chancellor of the University." *Cambridge Portfolio*, I, 111, 112 (1840).	

ACTOR-LISTS

Dr Boas, pp. 393–401, has given Actor-Lists for *Hymenæus, Richardus Tertius, Silvanus, Hispanus, Machiavellus, Leander* and *Labyrinthus*.

He has fallen into error in his identification of 'Howard' who played 'Eduardus Rex' in *Richardus Tertius*. In the Tanner MS. Howard appears as 'Dᵉ William Howard.' He was Lord William Howard, 'Belted Will.' In March 1578/9 he was a boy of 15 and therefore of right age to impersonate the boy-king.

We have lists also for the following performances: *Locus, Corpus, etc.,* 1604/5, *Zelotypus,* 1605/6, *Adelphe,* 1611/2, 1612/3, *Scyros,* 1612/3, *Melanthe,* 1614/5, *Ignoramus,* 1614/5, 1615, *Fraus Honesta,* 1618/9, *Loiola,* 1622/3, *Paria,* 1627/8, *Versipellis,* 1631/2, *The Rivall Friends,* 1631/2, *Valetudinarium,* 1637/8.

Locus, Corpus, etc.

Acted at Trinity College, 1604/5 (?). (From Tanner MS. 306)

Locus	Ds Moore	{Benedict Moore, schol. 1602, A.B. 1604/5 or Gabriel Moore, A.B. 1604/5
Corpus	Coote	Thomas Coote*, A.B. 1605/6
Motus	Cademan	Thomas Cademan, A.B. 1605/6
Tempus	Jorham	
Infinito	Mansell	John Mansell, A.M. Trin. 1609
Fimitum	Leedes	Sam. Leeds, schol. 1602, A.B. 1604/5
Vacuo	Stockdall	Jerem. Stockdall, A.B. 1605/6

(All of Trinity College)

Zelotypus

Acted at St John's College, 1605/6 (?). (From the Trinity and Emm. MSS.)

	Trin.	Em.	
Cassander	Mr Rollinson	Mr Rawlinson	Fras Rollinson*, A.M. 1598
Lavinia	Hinchman	Henchman	Ric. Henchman, A.B. 1605/6
Rupertus	Ds Smith		
Smeralda	Layfeild	Layfelde	Thos. Layfeild*, A.B. 1606/7

* Fellow of the college, then or subsequently.

Pueri Cass. filii {	Gibson	Storr	Abr. Gibson, A.B. 1606/7
	Store		Ben. Storr, A.B. 1608/9
Adrianus	Ds Miller	—	
Ferdinandus	Powell	Ds Powell	
Ascanius	Sampson	—	Ric. Sampson, A.B. 1605/6
Valerius	Mr Holt	Mr Houle	Jer. Holt*, A.M. 1603
Phanio	Mr Paramour	—	Thos. Parramore, fellow-commoner, matr. 1601
Pantaleo	Mr Clifton	—	Jervoise Clifton, fellow-commoner, matr. 1603
Elenchio	Mr Grace	—	Jo. Grace*, A.M. 1604
Trapula	Mr Taylor sen.	Mr Taylour iun.	Ric. Tailer*, A.M. 1597, Zac. Taylor, A.M. 1604
Cerberinus	Mr Layne	—	Rob. Lane*, A.M. 1600
Biberia	Mr Henshawe	Mr Haynshaw	? Thos. Henshaw*, A.B. 1606/7
Ludovicus	Mr Porter	Porter	Talbot Porter, A.B. 1605/6
Gloriano	Mr Casse	—	Edm. Casse*, A.M. 1603
Talanta	Barret	—	Will. Barrett, matr. 1604, A.B. 1607/8
Aurelia	Hubbersly	Habersley	
Mariscallus	Ds Maud	Ds Maude	Edw. Mawde, A.B. 1603/4
Gripus	Haslhurst	Haslehurste	Pet. Haslehurst, A.B. 1606/7
Congruo	Walton	—	Nich. Walton, matr. 1604, A.B. 1607/8
Lovarius	Fenston	Funston	Tho. Funston, A.B. 1606/7

(All of St John's College)

Adelphie

Acted at Trinity College, 1611/2 and 1612/3.   (From Trin. Coll. MS. R. 3. 9)

Cast of 1611/2:

Manlianus	Ds Coote	Will. Coote*, A.B. 1608/9, A.M. 1612
Fidelia	Mr Walpoole gen.	Joh. Walpoole, matr. f. c. 1610
Eroticus	Mr Chappell	Jo. Chappell*, A.M. 1611
Charitia	Titley sen.	? Pet. Titley, matr. 1612
Cannius	Hackett	Jo. Hackett*, A.B. 1612/3
Flammius	Mr Kinaston	Fra. Kinaston*, A.M. 1609
Sulpitia	Stubbs	Edm. Stubbs*, matr. 1610/1, A.B. 1614/5, A.M. 1618
Rosella	Fitzgefferye	Hen. Fitzgeofry, matr. 1611 (author of *Satyres and Satyricall Epigrams*, 1617)
Calpurnius	Ds Facon	Rob. Facon*, A.B. 1610/1
Cerinthus	Pearse	Steph. Pearse*, A.B. 1612/3
Martepalvenerius	Mr Sleepe	Ant. Sleepe*, A.M. 1609
Pythius	Mr Remington gen.	Rob. Barne Remington, matr. f. c. 1610
Albinus	Mr Coote	Tho. Coote*, A.M. 1609

Cast of 1612/3:

Manlianus	Ds Facon	See above
Charitia	Mr Butler	? Hen. Boteler, matr. f. c. 1612
Cannius	Ds Hackett	See above
Flammius	Mr Coote	[Prob. Will. Coote above]

Rosella	Dˢ Goldfinch	Tho. Goldfinch*, A.B. 1610/1
Calpurnius	Holmes	Geo. Holmes, matr. 1611
Cerinthus	Meredith	Rich. Meredith*, matr. 1612
Pythius	Dˢ Greeke	Tho. Greeke*, A.B. 1612/3
Albinus	Loyde	Rob. Loyd*, matr. 1612, A.B. 1615/6

(The other parts assigned as before)

Scyros

Acted at Trinity College, 1612/3. (From Trin. Coll. MS. R. 17. 10)

Orontes	Dˢ Facon	See *Adelphe*
Alcastus	Dˢ Goodin	Ralph Goodwin*, A.B. 1612/3
Orminus	Hackluit	Edm. Hakluit*, A.B. 1615/6, A.M. 1619
Syrenus	Dˢ Greeke	See *Adelphe*
Nisus	Mr Chappell	„
Armindus	Mr Coote jun.	„
Cœlia	Mr Walpoole	„
Chloris	Stubbs	„
Lycida	Dˢ Hakket	
Florinda	Chester	Granado Chester*, A.B. 1615/6
Elpinus	Mr Hunt	
Menalcas	Mr Sleepe	See *Adelphe*
Coccadorus	Dˢ Gooldfinch	„

Melanthe

Acted at Trinity College, 1614/5.	Mr Clarke	(From a MS. list in the Bodleian printed copy (1615)[1])
		Matth. Clark*, A.M. 1614
Palemon	Mr Clarke	
Serranus		
Montanus		
Melanthe	Mr Darci	Matr. f. c. E. 1615
Alcinus	Stubbs	See *Adelphe*
Alteus		
Melidorus	Mr Chapple	See *Adelphe*
Sylveria	Thorndick	Herbert Thorndick*, matr. 1613
Nicander	Mr Goldfinch	See *Adelphe*
Ermilia	Peake	Humph. Peake, matr. 1613
Glaucus	Simons	? Pet. Simon, matr. E. 1615
Leoniscus	Mr Sleepe	See *Adelphe*
Cervinus	Hakluit	See *Scyros*
Eccho		
Chorus		

1 Melanthe Fabula pastoralis acta cum Iacobus Cantabrigiam suam nuper inviseret; ibidemq: Musarum atque eius animi gratiâ dies quinque Commoraretur. Egerunt Alumni Coll. San. et Individuæ Trinitatis Cantabrigiæ. Excudebat Cantrellus Legge. Mart. 27, 1615.

Ignoramus

Acted at Trinity College, 1614/5.		(From Baker's list (based on Sancroft's) Harl. MS. 7042)
Theodorus	Mr Hutchinson Clar.	? Ja. H. Cla. A.M. 1600, S.T.B. 1608/9
Antonius	Mr Hollis Chr.	Denzil H. Chr. A.B. 1612/3, A.M. 1616, Baron Holles of Ifield, 1661
Ignoramus	Mr Perkinson Clar.	? Tho. P. Cla.*, A.B. 1607/8, A.M. 1611
Dulman	Mr Towers Qu.	John T. Qu.*, A.B. 1601/2, A.M. 1606, Bp. of Peterborough
Musæus	Mr Perient Clar.	? Humph. Periant Cla. matr. 1612 [no degree]
Pecus	Mr Parker Clar.	? Tho. P. Cla. A.M. 1605, or Will. P. Cla. A.B. 1612/3, A.M. 1616
Torcol	Mr Bargrave Clar.	Isaac B. A.M. (Pem.), 1610, S.T.P. (Cla.), 1621, Dean of Canterbury
Rosabella	Mr Morgan Qu.	Tho. M. Qu. matr. f. c. M. 1614, A.B. of Oxford
Surda	Mr Compton Qu.	Spencer C. Qu. matr. f. c. 1614, A.M. 1615, fil. nob. E. of Northampton
Trico	Mr Lake Clar.	Will. L. Cla. A.M. 1606
Bannacar	Ds Love Clar.	Ric. L. Cla.*, A.B. 1614/5, Master of C.C.C., Dean of Ely
Cupes	Mr Mason Pem.	? matriculated
Polla	Ds Chesham Clar.	Tho. C. Cla. A.B. 1613/4, A.M. 1617
Cola	Mr Wake G. & C.	Tho. W. Cai.*, A.M. 1606

Ignoramus (cont.)

Dorothea	Norfolk Qu.	? matriculated
Vince	Mr Compton Qu.	See above
Nell	Turner Clar.	Fra. T. Cla. A.B. 1614/5
Richardus	Grame Cla.	? matriculated
Pyropus	Mr Wake G. & C.	See above
Fidicen	Rinnarde Clar.	? Geo. Kennard Cla. matr. 1611, A.B. 1615/6, A.M. 1619
Nauta Gallicus	Thorogood Clar.	Fra. T. Cla. matr. 1612, A.B. 1615/6
Nauta Anglicus	Mr Mason Pem.	See above
Caupo	Thorogood Cla.	See above

J. S. Hawkins (*Ignoramus*, 1787, p. xxv), adds:

Characters in the Prologue, 1614/5:

Cursor	Mr Compton Qu.	See above
Equiso	Mr Mason Pem.	,,
Caballus (Davus Dromo)	Mr Lake Clar.	,,

[The prefix Mr seems in this list to be given irregularly to men who were neither Masters of Arts, nor Fellow-Commoners. We are not informed, I think, if the cast was changed for the performance of May 13th. A new prologue was then given, in which Puer Veredarius, Dulman, Ignoramus, Messe Davy, Lictores, Schioppius and Testis had parts: but the actors' names are not known.]

Fraus Honesta

Acted at Trinity College, 1618/9

(From Emm. Coll. MS. 3. 1. 17 and Trin. Coll. MS. R. 17. 10)

Cleomachus	Dˢ Loyde (Loide)	See *Adelphe*
Diodorus	Dˢ Fairfax (Fairefax)	Peregrine Fairfax, A.B. 1618/9
Callidamus	Mr Stubbe	See *Adelphe*
Ergasilus	Dˢ Hackluit (Hackluit)	See *Scyros*
Perillus	Vincent	Tho. Vincent*, matr. 1618, A.B. 1621/2, A.M. 1625
Chrisophilus	Mr Chauncy (Chancy)	Ch. Chauncy*, A.M. 1617
Cuculus	Dˢ Alcocke	Will. Alcocke, A.B. 1618/9
Onobarus	Dˢ Lawe	Matth. Lawe, A.B. 1617/8
Nitella	Valence	Joh. Valence, matr. 1617
Floretta	Drywood (Drywoode)	Geo. Drywood*, matr. 1618
Misogamus	Mr Delawne	
Canidia	Tutesham (Tatesham)	Zach. Tuttesham, A.B. 1619/20
Tres Vigiles	Elrington	Edw. Elrington, matr. 1617
	Cunningham	
	Blackhall (Blakehall)	Alex. Blackhall, matr. 1614

(The above names belong to Trinity College)

MS

6

Loiola

Acted at Trinity College, 1622/3.   (From Trin. Coll. MS. R. 17.9)

Gaudentius	Mr Rhodes	John Roades*, A.M. 1620
Philander	Thornton	Tho. Thornton*, A.B. 1623/4, A.M. 1627
Dromo	Edgly	Geo. Edgly, A.B. 1622/3
Martinus	Mr Alcock	W. Alcocke, A.M. 1622
Musonius	Powel	Tho. Powell, matr. E. 1622
Nebbia	Mr Goring	? Geo. Goring (no college specified), A.M. fil. nob. 1626
Mutus, seu } Faustina }	Mr Bulkley	
Acheron	Sr Mercer	Fra. Mercer, A.B. 1622/3, A.M. 1626
Lauerna	Harrison	Cha. Harrison, A.B. 1621/2
Scarabaeus	Mr Hackluit	See *Scyros*
Coelia	Mr Hinton	Sam. Hinton*, A.M. 1620
Jodocus	Sr Legat	John Legat, A.B. 1619/20
Mounsier } Michael }	Sr Hersent	Peter Hersent, A.B. 1620/1, A.M. 1624
Capitano } Vander Pons }	Cartwright	Tho. Cartwright, matr. 1621

κωφὰ πρόσωπα

Nicholaus } Machiauellus }	Mr Ran[cut off]	
Loiola	Mr Geares	
	[corrected to Hinton]? See above	
Xauerius	Sr Jones	Rob. Jones, A.B. 1620/1
Mariana	Priest	Hen. Priest, matr. 1622
Aquauiua	Mr Stasmore	
Personius	Mr Oxford	
Campianus	Mr Nelham	
Cæca Obedientia	Williams	
Pseudo miracu-} lum }	Mr Dalton	
Regicidium	Mr Coot	Chas. Coote, matr. f. c. 1622
Index Expurga-} torius }	Mr Goring	See above
Æquivocatio	Keamish	
Arrogantia	Harding	

(The actors, so far as traced, are of Trinity College. Many seem not to have matriculated)

Paria

Acted at Trinity College, 1627/8. (From Emm. Coll. MS. I. 3. 16)

Tiberius	Mr Bristoe	Litton Bristowe*, A.M. 1626
Astræa	Fotherbie	Thos. Fotherbie, matr. 1625, A.B. 1628/9, Cha. Fotherbe*, matr. 1627
Flauia	Bacon	
Lidonia	Shawe	Geo. Shawe*, matr. 1627, A.B. 1631/2
Archaicus	Mr Hearsante	See *Loiola*
Fuluus seu Fulgentius	Mr Thorneton	"
Lesbia	Winkefeilde	Tho. Wingfeld, matr. 1625
Petructius	munseye	Will. Munsey*, matr. 1626, A.B. 1629/30
Eleaser	Ds Loe	Will. Loe*, A.B. 1625/6
Nicholaus	Mr Wincop iu.	Joh. Whincopp*, A.M. 1625, Tho. Whincopp*, A.M. 1619
Iodocus	Mr Horseye	Geo. Horsey*, A.M. 1627
Babyla	Ds Swan	Joh. Swann, A.B. 1625/6, A.M. 1629
Phrygio	wiatte	Dudley Wyat*, matr. 1627, A.B. 1631/2
Asellio	Mr Mercer	See *Loiola*
Brylla	Rilye	Tho. Rylye*, matr. 1626
Mysis	Snead	Will. Sneade, matr. 1626
Authore T. Vincent		See *Fraus Honesta*

(All of Trinity College)

Versipellis

Acted at Queens' College, 1631/2 (?)

(From a MS. among the papers of Rev. T. Pestell the elder, possibly the author. J. Nichols' *Leicestershire*, III, 927)

Dˢ Bryant	Ric. Bryan*, A.B. 1627/8, A.M. 1631, Oliver Brian, A.B. 1628/9, A.M. 1632
Flout	Joh. Flote, matr. 1631, A.B. 1634/5 (Float)
Dˢ Woodhall	? Horat. Woodhouse, A.B. 1630/1
Dˢ Bea-	? Edw. Beale, A.B. 1629/30
Richards	
Freear	Mich. Freear*, A.B. 1633/4, A.M. 1637
Dˢ Rogers	Sam. Rogers*, A.B. 1630/1
Mr Harflett	Cha. Harflet, A.B. 1628/9, A.M. 1632
Jocelin	Sim. Jocelin, A.B. 1632/3
Overton	Ric. Overton, matr. 1631
Mr Kemp	Edw. Kemp, A.B. 1628/9, A.M. 1632
Mr Rogers	Joh. Rogers*, A.M. 1631
Dˢ Cantrell	Tho. Cantrell, A.B. 1629/30
Ramsbottom	Tho. Ramsbottom, matr. 1629, A.B. 1632/3
Dˢ Johnson	Will. Johnson, A.B. 1630/1, A.M. 1634
Hemson	

Versipellis (cont.)

Bradler   ? Pet. Bradlie, matr. 1629
Wills   Will. Wells, A.B. 1633/4, A.M. 1637
Ds Carlisle Tho. Carleill, A.B. 1631/2
Penson
Pestell   Tho. Pestell, A.B. 1632/3, A.M. 1636
Ds Allen sen. Rob. Allen, A.B. 1631/2
Crofts   Leon. Crofts, matr. 1629

(All of Queens' College)

The Rivall Friends

Acted by Queens' College men, 19th March, 1631/2

(From a cast in the B.M. copy of the book (1632), 644, b. 45, which belonged to Thos. Alston, Qu., A.B. 1629/30, A.M. 1633)

S. Hooke   Mr Richard Brian socius See *Versipellis*
Pandora   Mannering
Mistris Vrsely Romsbotom   See *Versipellis*
Iacke Loueall   Sr Rogers   Sam. Rogers*. See *Versipellis*
Constantina   [S]r Lin.

Role	Actor	Note
Lucius	Mr Kempe	See *Versipellis*
Lively	Mr Stanninow	Jas. Stanino (Stanenough)*, A.M. 1629
Terpander	Sr Hills	Ralph Hills, A.B. 1629/30, Heigham Hills*, A.B. 1631/2, A.M. 1635
Anteros	Mr Hausted	Pet. Hausted, A.B. 1623/4 A.M. 1627
Laurentio	Sr Cantrel	Tho. Cantrell, A.B. 1629/30, A.M. 1633
Endymion	Mr Cotterel	? Chas. Cottrell, matr. f. c. 1629
Isabella	Freer	See *Versipellis*
Stipes	Mr John Rogers	„
Placenta	Piercen	„
Merda	Tiffin	Benj. Tiffin, matr. 1631, A.B. 1634/5
Nodle Emptie	Mr Harflet Inceptr	Cha. Harflet. See *Versipellis*
W. Wiseacres	Mr Hards	Pet. Hardresse*, A.B. 1626/7, A.M. 1630
Mr Mungrell	Sr Woodhouse	Horat. W. See *Versipellis*
Hammershin	Hausted	Will. Hawsted, matr. 1629, A.B. 1632/3
Z. Knowlittle	Kidbie	Joh. Kidby, matr. 1629, A.B. 1633/4
T. All-mouth	Richardson	Jos. Richardson, matr. 1629, A.B. 1632/3
S. Legg	Sr Carlile	See *Versipellis*
S. Fillpot	Hills	See above
H. Obligation	? Slater	Edw. Slater, A.B. 1632/3
The Authour	Pet. Hausted	See above

(All of Queens' College)

Valetudinarium

Acted at Queens' College 1637/8?.   (From St John's Coll. Camb. MS. S. 59)

Algidius	Mr Wells	See *Versipellis*
Minulus	Marsh	Rich. March or Marsh, matr. 1637, A.B. 1640/1
Mirabella	Mr Frear	See *Versipellis*
Archiater	Ds Jones	John Jones, A.B. 1635/6, A.M. 1639
Urinulus	Richardson	John R. matr. 1637, A.B. 1640/1
Nonaria	Lightfoot	Geo. L. matr. 1637, A.B. 1640/1
Winifreda	Maldon	Dan. Malden, matr. 1637, A.B. 1640/1
Magnificus	Mr Johnson	See *Versipellis*
Ucalegon	Ds Whitloe	Edw. Whitlowe, A.B. 1636/7, A.M. 1640
Cordelia	Whitehead	Jasper Whithead*, matr. 1636, A.B. 1639/40
Perilupus	Ds Stanhop	Geo. Stanhope, A.B. 1635/6, A.M. 1639
Bubonius	Ds Lynsell	Tho. Lindsell, A.B. 1635/6, A.M. 1639
Theotimus	Ds Sleighton	Rob. S. A.B. 1637/8, A.M. 1641
Pythiolus	Mr Rogers	Sam. R.*; see *Versipellis*
Ipswichus	Mr Walpole	Art. Walpole*, A.B. 1632/3, A.M. 1636
Linna	Sandall	Benj. Sandall, matr. 1634, A.B. 1640/1
Molossus	Mr Pestill	Thos. Pestell, A.B. 1632/3, A.M. 1636
Coquus	Whiniate	Rob. Whinyats, matr. 1635, A.B. 1638/9
Autore Mro Johnson		See above

(All of Queens' College)

BIBLIOGRAPHICAL NOTES

I SUBMIT some notes (1) on the Cambridge plays mentioned in the *Cambridge History of English Literature*, vol. VI, bibliography to chapter XII, pp. 468–87, and (2) on Cambridge plays not there mentioned.

W. Alabaster:

Roxana. Query, acted at Trinity College, *c.* 1590–1595?

S. Brooke:

Adelphe. Acted at Trinity College in 1611/2, 1612/3, 1662 and May 1669.

The performance in 1612/3 before Prince Charles and the Prince Palatine took place apparently on March 4th, that of *Scyros* on March 3rd. These dates are reversed in the *Retrospective Review* and Cooper.

The college accounts, May 1669, 'for painting NOLA upon the stage' suggest a performance then.

The Trin. Coll. MS. R. 3. 9 gives author, dates, and casts for 1611/2 and 1612/3, R. 10. 4 the prologue and epilogue for 1662.

Melanthe. Performed at Trinity, March 10th, 1614/5. A copy of the printed play (1615) in the Bodleian contains the cast in MS.

Scyros. See above under *Adelphe.*

To the MSS. mentioned, add Trin. Coll. R. 10. 4 which gives the cast and date '3⁰ mens. Mart. 1612.' The '3⁰' was misread '30' and so appears in Trin. Coll. MS. R. 3. 9 and Emm. Coll. MS. 3. 1. 17.

Perhaps acted again on 24th March, 1613/4.

In the last scene we have Orontes, etc., 'cum cantilena triumphali.' Mr Aldis Wright ingeniously suggested that this was the basis of the mythical MS. play 'Catilina Triumphans' said to be preserved at Trinity.

A. Cowley:

The Guardian. The Prologue and Epilogue in Harl. MS. 6918, fo. 25v, Egerton MS. 2725, fo. 31, Douce MS. 357, Rawl. Poet. MS. 26, fo. 138.

The title in the Douce MS. is 'The Prologue and Epilogue in a Comedy made by ye Poet Aquila pʳsented att ye Entertainmᵗ of the Princes Highñss by the Schollars of Trinity Colledge in Cambridge March 1641.' At the side, explanatory of 'ye Poet Aquila,' is written 'Pooly,' probably for 'Cooly.'

Naufragium Joculare. For 'Nonas' read '4⁰ Nonas' (sc. 2 Feb.). The year 1638 means I suppose 1638/9 (so the *Retrospective Review*): Fleay takes it as 1638, perhaps because the printed copy is dated 1638. But this might well have been got out between 2 Feb. and 25 March.

Aquila Cruso:

Euribates. Query, acted at Caius in 1615/6? Aquila Cruso was A.B. 1613/4, A.M. 1618.

Ph. Fletcher:

Sicelides. Acted at King's, 11 March, 1614/5.

A. Fraunce:

Victoria. Query, acted at St John's, 1578/9 or Christmas 1579?

W. Goldingham:

Herodes. Query, at Trinity Hall, *c.* 1570–75?

J. Hacket:

Loiola. Acted at Trinity College on Feb. 28, and (before King James) on March 12, 1622/3.

Trin. Coll. MS. R. 17. 9 gives the cast, and the two prologues. The B.M. Add. MS. 26709 belonged once to Vincent Freeman of Emm. Coll. A.B. 1625/6. A fourth MS. among the Durham Cathedral Hunter MSS. (quarto 26. 1).

Verses on *Loiola* by 'M. Gunne' (? 'M Gwine') dated 'M. id.' (15th March) in MS. Rawl. Poet. 117, fo. 25: others by 'F. K.' at end of Trin. Coll. MS. R. 17. 9.

P. Hausted:

The Rivall Friends. Acted at Queens' College (or, if we may disregard the title-page, at Newmarket), 19 March, 1631/2. As there is no record of a royal visit to Cambridge before that of March 22nd, Cooper[1] supposes that *two* comedies were acted on that day. But that is out of the question. T. Randolph in his *Oratio Prævaricatoria* of July 1632 referred to the play as already published:

[1] *Annals,* III, 249, 250.

Illa res comica, quæ primò ante Regem acta est, *amicos* habuit, sed sine *Rivalibus*. Fuit optima comœdia a priori, sed olet a posteriori. Nunc impressa est. Miror ego ejus hominis stomachum qui talem librum edere potuit. Ego in illius laudes sic cecini : Jam sileat Jack Drum : taceat miracula Tom Thumb.

A copy of the printed book in the B.M. (644 b 45) contains the cast in MS. It belonged to Thos. Alston, Queens' (A.M. 1633).

Senile Odium. Query, acted at Queens' College, 1628/9 or 1630/1 ? Kemp's introductory verses speak of it as 'primogenitum Autoris.' Hence, though printed a year later, it may have been produced earlier than *The Rivall Friends.*

Randolph's *Orat. Prævaricatoria*, 1632, has some cryptic allusions to Ward's *Fucus* and this play :

Ignavum fucus pecus est, petit illico lucos :
Et factus blancum non saltat prinkum prankum.
Dicunt hoc puerile *Odium* vicisse *Senile*,
Hic est sensus non, et possis ludere *checkstone.*

There is a MS. of the play in the Marquis of Bath's collection at Longleat. (*Hist. MSS. Comm. App. to 3rd Report*, p. 200.)

W. Hawkesworth :

Labyrinthus. Neither Trin. Coll. MS. R. 2. 6 nor Douce MS. 43 contains this play. Acted at Trinity College at the Bachelor's Commencement 1602/3, and in 1622/3 before King James. Most MSS. give the cast of 1602/3. The division of the persons of the drama into houses given in some MSS. is imperfectly given in the printed book.

Leander. Acted in 1598 (? 1597/8) and 1602/3.
The Prologue to the performance of 1602/3 was
used also for *Pastor Fidus.*

W. Johnson:
Valetudinarium. Acted at Queens' College, 6 Feb.
1637/8. St John's Coll. MS. S. 59 gives the whole
play, but in two hands. It also gives the cast.

The author W. Johnson (see Searle's *History of
Queens' College,* pp. 515, 516) is wrongly described
in the Emm. and St John's MSS. as a *fellow* of the
college.

T. Kirchmayer:
Pammachius. Acted at Christ's College in 1544/5.

T. Legge:
Richardus Tertius. Acted at St John's ? 1578/9,
? 1582/3, ? 1586/7. The Camb. Univ. Lib. MS.
is dated 'Comitii Bacchal. 1579.' As a rule one
would interpret this date as = March 1579/80.

The evidence of the St John's accounts would
point to the date 1578/9. Possibly the Bachelor's
Commencement was held after the 25th March,
which would render the date '1579' correct.

Another MS. of the play is in the Hatton collection.
(See *Hist. MSS. Comm. App. to 1st Report,* p. 32 b.)

The *D.N.B.* speaks of one in the Phillipps collection.

Destruction of Jerusalem. A play with this title is
credited to Legge by Fuller.

P. Mease:

Adrastus parentans. Query, acted at Jesus College, *c.* 1618–27?

W. Mewe:

Pseudomagia. Query, acted at Emmanuel College, *c.* 1625?

T. Randolph:

Aristippus. At Trinity College, *c.* 1626–31.

A MS. with interesting variants from the printed text in MS. Sloan 2531, 16.

The Conceited Peddler. At Trinity College, *c.* 1626–31.

The Jealous Lovers. At Trinity College, before the King and Queen, 22 March 1631/2.

The Muses Looking-Glasse (originally called 'The Entertainment'). At Trinity College, 1626–31.

Hey for Honesty, Down with Knauery. ? At Trinity, 1626–31. No mention is made in the *Cambridge History* Bibliography of this work:

Πλουτοφθαλμία Πλουτογαμία. A pleasant Comedie, Entituled Hey for Honesty, Down with Knauery. Translated out of Aristophanes his Plutus, by Tho: Randolph. Augmented and Published by F. J. 1651.

The work is far more than a translation. Though the *D.N.B.* questions Randolph's authorship, internal evidence seems to me to confirm the statement of the title-page. Compare the reference to Maxentius, in *Randolph's Works*, ed. Hazlitt, p. 467 with that on p. 540.

J. Rickets:

Byrsa Basilica. ? At Jesus College, *c.* 1633.
The play contains a document 'acta di: 20 Aug.
1633.' (See Boas, *Univ. Drama*, p. 132 *n.*) John
Ricketts; Jesus, A.B. 1625/6, A.M. 1629.

T. Riley (?):

Cornelianum Dolium. I see no reason for doubting
that the London publisher who appended to this
work the words 'Auctore T.R. ingeniosissimo hujus
ævi Heliconis' meant to suggest that the work was
written by Randolph. Randolph's work, *The Muses
Looking-Glasse,* bore on its title-page 'By T.R.
Oxford. . 1638.' If the work is not by Randolph, one
need not search for an author bearing his initials.
That the play belongs to Cambridge is shown by
the words in Act IV, Sc. 6, 'in Anatis Vico,' i.e. in
Duck Lane. Cp. the reference in Randolph's *The
Conceited Peddler* (Hazlitt, I, 40).

G. Ruggle:

Ignoramus. At Trinity, 8 March 1614/5, 13 May
1615. The play occurs twice in Tanner MS. 306.
It is found in Douce MS. 43. The cast is given in
Add. MS. 4457, fo. 16 (a copy of that in Baker's
hand in Harl. MS. 7042).
Re Vera or Verily (now lost) and *Club Law* (q.v.)—
both English comedies—are credited to Ruggle in
a MS. note made in 1751 in a copy of *Ignoramus*
by John Hayward, M.A., Clare Hall.

J. Sadler:

Masquerade du Cul. Probably never acted, nor intended for acting.

J. Simeon. It is most unlikely that any of these plays were acted at Cambridge. The words 'anno 1631 acta' on the Camb. Univ. Lib. MS. of *Zeno,* which misled the writer of the article in *Retrospective Review,* xii, p. 5, no doubt refer to Douay or some other place abroad.

Another MS. of *Zeno* in St John's Coll. Camb. (James' *Catalogue,* no. 504).

T. Sparrowe:

Confessor. ? Acted at St John's, *c.* 1634.

W. Stevenson:

Gammer Gurton's Needle. ? Acted at Christ's College, 1553/4.

If the play was written wholly or in part by Bridges (Boas, *Un. Drama,* p. 83), W. Stevenson was still probably responsible for its production.

E. Stub:

Fraus Honesta. Acted at Trinity College, 10 Feb. 1618/9 and 24 Sept. 1629 (see Cooper, *Annals,* iii, 219).

The play in Harl. MS. 2296, fo. 151, called *Callidamus et Callanthia* on p. 483 of the *Camb. Hist.,* is *Fraus Honesta.*

T. Tomkis:

Albumazar. At Trinity Coll., 9 March, 1614/5.

Lingua. ? Acted at Trinity, *c.* 1602 and *c.* 1616.

A Dutch translation of the play by Lambert van den Bos (or Bosch) 1648.

Are *Locus, Corpus, etc., Pathomachia, Band, Cuffe and Ruffe,* and *Worke for Cutlers* by the same author?

N. Udall:

Ezechias. Acted in King's Coll. Chapel, 8th Aug. 1564.

T. Vincent:

Paria. Acted at Trinity Coll., 3rd March, 1627/8.

The Emm. MS. contains the cast. The *Retros. Review's* statement that it was acted again in 1641/2 appears to be groundless. The play is based on Eusebio Luchetti's *Le due Sorelle Rivali*—Venice 1609.

R. Ward:

Fucus Histriomastix. Acted at Queens' Coll., 1622/3 and a few weeks later before the King at Newmarket.

H. Molle's verses are found in Rawlinson MSS. Poet. 147 and 210.

For Randolph's reference, see P. Hausted, *Senile Odium, sup.*

T. Watson:

Absalon. Acted at St John's Coll., *c.* 1535–44.

It has been said that there is a MS. at Penshurst. It apparently is not now to be found there.

M S

7

N. Wilbourne:

Machiavellus. Acted at St John's Coll., 9 Dec. 1597. The Douce MS. contains the cast.

[A. Wingfield]:

Pedantius. Acted at Trinity Coll., probably Feb. 1581. For proof that the author was Edward Forset see *Times Literary Supplement,* 10 Oct. 1918.

Authors Unknown

Andronicus Comnenus. Acted at Magdalen Coll. Oxford, 26 Jan. 1617/8. By Samuel Bernard, Master of Magdalen School, and afterwards Vicar of Croydon. So not a Cambridge play.

Antoninus Bassianus Caracalla. ? Acted at Cambridge.

Band, Cuffe and Ruffe. ? Acted at Trinity College, Cambridge, 1614/5. It was entered on the Stationers' Register, 10 Feb. 1614/5. The second edition (*Exchange Ware, etc.*) has a number of short poems at the beginning.

Among the MSS. of Matt. Wilson, Esq., Eshton Hall, Yorks., is, or was, 'A comedy with prologue and epilogue dated Oxford, Feb. 24, 1646. The actors are Band, Ruff and Cuff, 6 pp.' (*Hist. MSS. Comm. App. to 3rd Report,* p. 295, vol. xvii.) This MS. appears to have been known to the editor who reprinted *Exchange Ware* in the *Harleian Miscellany.* See under T. Tomkis, *sup.*

Callidamus et Callanthia. See under E. Stub above.

Cancer. Probably a Cambridge play, as it was printed in 1648 with *Loiola* (Trin.), *Stoicus Vapulans* (St John's, Xmas 1618), *Paria* (Trinity, 1627/8).

Based on Lionardo Salviati's *Il Granchio* of which a second edition appeared with the same author's *La Spina* at Florence in 1606 (*Due Commedie, etc.*).

Club Law. See under G. Ruggle.

Clytophon. Probably a Cambridge play. The Emmanuel MS. belonged to William Breton, Fellow of Emmanuel (A.M. 1625).

Exchange Ware. See under *Band, Cuffe and Ruffe.*

Fatum Vortigerni. ? Acted at Cambridge, *c.* 1595–1600.

Fortunia. See under *Susenbrotus.*

Fraus Pia. One would put the play about 1643 ('Smectymnuus') if the words 'gratias Amnestiæ' did not suggest a post-Restoration production. Possibly a play written for a school ('anhelantibus puerum conatibus').

Hispanus. Acted at St John's College, 1596/7.

[*Hymenæus.*] Probably by A. Fraunce or H. Hickman.

[*Jovis et Junonis nuptiæ.*] Possibly acted at Cambridge.

Lælia. Acted at Queens' Coll. 1546 (?) and 1595 (?). From an item in the Queens' Coll. accounts for 1546, 'New made garmentes at the comœdie of Lælia Modenas,' it would seem that the play dates from that time. In that case the Latin would be based on C. Estiennes' *Le Sacrifice* (1543) rather than on one of the later editions of this play called *Les Abusez* (1549 and 1556).

[*Nottola.*] Possibly acted at Cambridge.

The *Parnassus* Trilogy. Acted at St John's, query, 1598/9, 1600/1 and 1602/3. See W. Lühr, *Die drei Cambridger Spiele vom Parnass* (Kiel dissertation, 1900). Add further to the bibliography: G. C. Moore Smith, 'The Parnassus Plays' (*Modern Language Review*, x, 162).

Parthenia. Probably acted at Cambridge some time after 1576.

Pastor Fidus. Acted at King's College. The Trinity MS. gives the play with the Prologue used in the 2nd version of W. Hawkesworth's *Leander*, 1602/3.

Pathomachia. If acted, acted at Trinity Coll., *c.* 1617? See under T. Tomkis, *sup.* The Harl. MS. 6869 is inscribed 'For Sʳ Robert Filmer in Westminster.' R. F. matric. Trin. Coll. 5 July 1604, knighted at Newmarket, 24 Jan. 1618/9.

Perfidus Hetruscus. Possibly a Cambridge play.

Romeus et Julietta. Possibly a Cambridge play.

Sapientia Solomonis. Acted at Trinity College, 1559/60. Query, also 1565/6?

The B.M. manuscript has an epilogue for a performance in 1565/6 by Westminster boys. The performance is attested (see a letter to *The Observer*, Dec. 1919) by the Abbey Muniments. So writes Dr Boas. This MS. was purchased at the Pickering sale, 12 Dec. 1854. Fleay mentions a MS. in the Bright sale, No. 225.

Silvanus. Acted at St John's Coll., 13 Jan. 1596/7 according to the Douce MS. The cast there given agrees better with the date 1597/8.

Solymannidæ. Acted at Cambridge. ? Date, 5 March 1581/2. The probable source is N. à Moffan's 'Soltani Solymanni..horrendum facinus..scelerato in..filium..Mustapham parricidio A.D. 1553 patratum,' 1555. (See J. W. Cunliffe, *Early English Classical Tragedies*, p. lvi.)

Stoicus Vapulans. Acted at St John's at Christmas, 1618.

Susenbrotus. From the date of a letter in the play, '12 die Martii 1615,' one assumes that the play was acted at Trinity on 12 March 1615/6. It is possible that the note on the MS. 'acta..in Collegio Trin.' is inexact, and that this was the play acted before the King at Royston. (Cooper, *Annals*, III, 102.) The Trinity accounts confirm this: 'To Mr Chappell for..necessaries for the Comedy to be acted at Court'...'To Mr Chappell going to the Court to see the comedy acted.'

It is possible that John Chappell, Fellow of Trinity, A.M. 1611, was the author of the play.

Timon. Possibly a Cambridge play. Dated by Fleay 1601.

Worke for Cutlers. ? At Trinity College, 1614/5. See T. Tomkis. Entered on the Stationers' Register, 4 July 1615.

Zelotypus. Acted at St John's College (Christmas, 1605?). Possibly both this and *Silvanus* were by Francis Rollinson, or Rawlinson, who took the chief role in each play. There is a MS. of the play (without cast) in Durham Cathedral MS. Hunter 76. 6.

Not in the *Cambridge History*.

Aristophanes:

Pax. Acted in Greek at Trinity Coll. 1546.

Plutus. Acted in Greek at St John's Coll. 1536.

T. Artour:

Two plays, *Microcosmus* and *Mundus Plumbeus*, by T. A., Fellow of St John's, 1520–32, are referred to by Bale, *Cent.* IX, 16 (both now lost).

R. Ascham:

Philoctetes. Ascham writes to Archbishop Lee in 1543 (*Letters*, ed. Giles, I, 32), that he had written a play based on Sophocles' *Philoctetes* in imitation of Seneca. If Lee permits, 'in tuo nomine divulgata apparebit.'

J. Barnes:

The Academie or The Cambridge Dunns. A Comedy. Acted (? at Emmanuel), 28 June 1675 and 26 June 1676. Emm. Coll. MS. III, I, 4 (two copies). In Act v 'to this present day and houre June 26 betweene ye houres of 7 and 8 at night Anno 1676' (other MS., 'June 28..1675').

Englebert. An Opera and Tragedy. ? Acted. Emm. Coll. MS. III, I, 2.

Landgartha, or the Amazon Queen of Denmark and Norway. 'An enterteinment Design'd for their Royal Highnesses The Prince and Princess of Denmark.' ? Acted. Emm. Coll. MS. III, 1, 2.

Emm. Coll. MS. III, 1, 4 contains an earlier draft entitled *Sigward ye famous K. of Norway* (finished 29 May 1682). T.R.H. were married 28 July 1683.

Plautus his Trinummi imitated (Comedy in English prose). ? Acted. Emm. Coll. MS. III, 1, 2. Date 1693.

T. Browne:

Thebais. A tragedy. ? Acted at Cambridge.

Thomas Browne, M.A., King's College, headmaster of Westminster, 1564–70.

[G. Buchanan?]:

Baptistes. John babtiste acted at Trinity Coll. 1562/3.

Jephthes. Acted at Trinity Coll. 1566/7.

Ascham, who was engaged on the *Scholemaster* till his death 30 Dec. 1568, implies that he had seen Buchanan's *Jephthes* acted (*Scholemaster*, ed. Mayor, p. 169). This was perhaps the occasion, unless the play had also been acted earlier. It was written *c.* 1540.

T. Cecill:

Æmilia. Acted at Trinity by members of St John's College on 7 March 1614/5. See Cooper, *Ann.* III, 71. (Play lost.)

J. Christopherson:

Jephthes [in Greek and Latin]. Boas (*Un. Drama*, p. 47) suggests that it was composed *c.* 1544 and perhaps never acted.

The Greek play Ιεφθαε is preserved in Trin. Coll. Camb. MS. O. 1. 37, dedicated to W. Parr, Earl of Essex, and in St John's Coll. MS. 284, dedicated to Cuthbert [Tunstall] Bishop of Durham.

The Latin version had been seen by Tanner (*Bibliotheca*).

Christopherson, an original Fellow of Trinity, 1546, was abroad from ? 1547 to 1553 when he became Master of Trinity.

W. Gnapheus (or Fullonius):

Acolastus. Acted at Trinity Coll. 1560/1.

Hypocrisis. Acted at Queens' Coll. 1548/9. Publ. 1544. See Creizenach, *Geschichte*, ii, 159.

E. Halliwell:

Dido. Acted in King's Coll. Chapel before the Queen by King's College men on 7 Aug. 1564. [Lost.]

B. Jonson:

The Silent Woman. Acted at Trinity Coll. in 1661/2 according to the epilogue to *Adelphe*.

There is an allusion in the epilogue of *The Silent Woman* to its having been acted at Oxford in the summer of 1673 (Lawrence, *Elizabethan Playhouse*, p. 214). It was acted in London in 1661 (see p. 15 *n.*).

Ph. Kynder:

Silvia. ? Acted. The play is lost.

Philip Kynder, Pembroke Hall, A.B. 1615/6. His book, MS. Ashmol. 788, fo. 205, has: 'This Epistle prefixt before my Siluia a latin comedie or pastorall translated from yᵉ Archadia written at 18 yeeres of age.' The Epistle consists of a string of Latin quotations. The name of the patron to whom it is addressed is left blank.

G. Macropedius:

Asotus. Acted at Trinity Coll. 1565/6.

T. May:

Julius Cæsar. Latin Tragedy. ? Acted at Sidney Sussex Coll. *c.* 1616. 'The original MS. of this play, which is in five short acts, is in the possession of Mr Stephen Jones' (Baker, *Biog. Dram.* 1812, II, p. 437).

T. Nashe (and another):

Terminus et non terminus. Acted at St John's Coll. ? 1585/6. [So stated in the *Trimming of Thomas Nashe.* See *Nashe's Works* (ed. M'Kerrow), v, 9.]

R. Nevile:

The Poor Scholar. A comedy written by Robert Nevile, Fellow of King's Colledge in Cambridge. 4°. London, 1662. ? Acted.

R. Nevile, A.B. 1660/1, M.A. 1664. The comedy is in prose, printed to the end of Act I, Sc. 4, as verse. It refers to college whippings taking place in the buttery, the victim lying on a barrel.

Plautus:

Pœnulus. At Queens' Coll. 1548/9.
Menechmus. At Trinity Coll. 1551/2 and 1565/6.
Stichus. At Queens', 1553/4; at Trinity, 1564/5.
Mostellaria. At Trinity Coll. 1559/60.
Amphitruo. At Trinity Coll. 1560/1.
Curculio. At Jesus Coll. 1562/3.
Pseudolus. At Trinity, 1562/3.
Trinummus. At Trinity, 1563/4.
Bacchides. At Trin. Coll. 1563/4; at Jesus, 1579.
Aulularia. At King's, Aug. 1564.
Asinaria. At Trin. 1565/6.
Persa. At Queens', 1547/8; at St John's, 1583.

[C. Roilletus]:

Philanira. Acted at Trinity Coll. 1564/5.

[The B.M. copy of *Claudii Roilleti..varia poemata*, Paris, 1556 (840 a 2) has the autograph 'Edoardus Mychelborn. 1586,' i.e. E. M. of Gloucester Hall, Oxford, the Latin poet, and friend of T. Campion and C. FitzGeoffrey.]

Seneca:

? *Troades*. At Trin. Coll. 1551/2 and 1560/1.
? *Oedipus*. At Trin. Coll. 1559/60.
? *Medea*. At Trin. Coll. 1560/1.

Chr. Smart:

A Trip to Cambridge, or The Grateful Fair. Acted at Pembroke Hall, *c*. 1745–7. A sketch of the contents and the cast is given in *The Poems of..Chr. Smart*, Reading, 1791, vol. I, pp. xii–xvi.

Terence:

Adelphi. At Queens' Coll. 1547/8; at Jesus Coll. 1562/3; at Trinity Coll. 1562/3.

Phormio. At Trinity Coll. 1562/3.

Eunuchus. At Jesus Coll. 1563/4.

(?) *Andria.* At Trinity Coll. 1609/10.

R. Textor:

Thersites. Acted apparently at Queens' Coll. in 1542/3.

T. Watson:

Antigone (translated from Sophocles). Acted at Cambridge, apparently in G. Harvey's time. He speaks in his MS. notes on Gascoigne of 'Vatsoni Antigone, magnificè acta solenni ritu, et verè tragico apparatu: cum pulcherrimis etiam pompis, et accuratissimis thematibus' (G. Harvey's *Marginalia*, p. 166). The translation was published: *Sophoclis Antigone interprete T. Watsono*, 1581.

[? H. Ziegler]:

Heli. Acted at Queens' Coll. 26 Jan. 1547/8.

Anon.

Anglia Deformata & Anglia Restituta, a show given at Trinity College at Christmas, 1553. [Lost.]

The Birthe of Hercules (based on Plautus'*Amphitruo*). ? Acted at Christ's College, *c.* 1598.

B.M. Add. MS. 28722. Edited by M. W. Wallace, Chicago, 1903, and by R. Warwick Bond, *Malone Society's Reprints*, 1911.

Perhaps by Richard Bernard, the translator of Terence, A.M. Christs' Coll. 1598. A defence of translation and reference to the fact that Terence was himself a translator occurs in the Prologue here as in Bernard's *Terence*, 'Ad Lectorem.'

Marcus Tullius Cicero. ? A Cambridge play. *The Tragedy of that Famous Roman Oratour Marcus Tullius Cicero*, 1651. (In English, blank-verse and rimed couplets.)

Attributed by Phillips (*Theatrum Poetarum*) and Winstanley to Fulk Greville, Lord Brooke. This attribution was denied by Langbaine. Mr W. Aldis Wright suggested, with little reason, Dr S. Brooke, author of *Adelphe*, *Melanthe* and *Scyros*.

De crumena perdita. Produced by M. Hutton (probably its author) at Trinity College in 1554/5. *Crumenaria* acted at the same college in 1565/6 was probably the same play. [Lost.]

Duns Furens. Acted at Peterhouse when Dr Perne was Vice-Chancellor or Deputy V.-C., i.e. probably either in 1580/1 or 1586/7. T. Nashe in *Have with you* (*Nashe's Works*, ed. M'Kerrow, iii, 80). [Lost.]

[*Locus, Corpus, etc.*] (In English.) Acted at Trinity College, *c.* 1604/5.

Bodleian, Tanner MS. 306, fo. 240 (imperfect), with cast. See T. Tomkis, *sup.*

[*Microcosmus.*] Latin. Acted at Trinity College?

Trin. Coll. MS. R. 10. 4. This is certainly a Cambridge play; cp. iii, 3, 'in nundinis..Sturbrigiensibus.' Its reference to the abundance of food in

Virginia and the absence of fasts points to a date later
than 1612.

Puer vapulans. The Jesus Coll. accounts for
1581–82 have the item 'Paid to Mr Murgetrod for
puer vapulans,' which would appear to have been
a play produced by Michael Murgetrode, Fellow of
the college (A.M. 1580). [Lost.]

Pygmalion. ? A Cambridge play.
MS. Rawl. D. 317, fo. 190. (Latin.) Only 260
lines, but complete with Epilogue.

Senilis Amor. ? Acted 4th Feb. 1635/6. Was it
written by Peter Hausted, the author of *Senile
Odium*, and therefore acted at Queens' College?
Bodleian MS. Rawlinson, Poet. 9. The MS. dates
the play '1635.' It is imperfect and arranged in
perturbed order. A missing scene is sketched in
another hand, with the note, 'this sceane full of
sport was basely torne out of this place.'

Sophomorus. ? Acted at Cambridge, 1620/1.
Hazlitt, following Halliwell, says that a play of this
name was 'formerly in the Bliss collection.' It is not
now in the Bliss collection at the Bodleian. The play
was dated '1620.' That it was a Cambridge play
seems evident, as the term 'sophomore' was only
used at Cambridge.

Tarrarantantara turba, &c. A show at Clare Hall,
c. 1581–6. [Lost.] So says T. Nashe in *Have with you*
(*Nashe's Works*, ed. M'Kerrow, III, 80), but perhaps
he is merely joking.

Versipellis. Acted at Queens' College, 1631/2?

Our knowledge of this lost play comes from
J. Nichols' *Leicestershire*, III, 927. In giving an
account of the poetical work of the Rev. Thos.
Pestell who in 1644 resigned the living of Packington
to his son the Rev. Thos. Pestell the younger, Nichols
says:

'I have now before me a volume of MS. poems by
Mr Pestell among which is a Latin comedy dated 1631
under the title Versipellis which appears to have been
acted (probably at Cambridge) by the following.' (Here
follows the cast given on p. 85.) 'The scene is at
Antwerp.'

Among the actors, who are all Queens' men, is
Thomas Pestell the younger, then an undergraduate.
According to Nichols, it was the father who wrote the
play (whose date is confirmed by the designations
of the actors) for performance at his son's college.
Otherwise one might have attributed it either to Peter
Hausted or to W. Johnson the author of *Valetu-
dinarium* who was one of the actors.

CAMBRIDGE : PRINTED BY THE SYNDICS OF THE UNIVERSITY PRESS

For EU product safety concerns, contact us at Calle de José Abascal, 56–1°,
28003 Madrid, Spain or eugpsr@cambridge.org.

www.ingramcontent.com/pod-product-compliance
Ingram Content Group UK Ltd.
Pitfield, Milton Keynes, MK11 3LW, UK
UKHW012337130625
459647UK00009B/352